For Reals! Observations by a Brown Guy

Gil Polanco

ISBN-10:1539389294
ISBN-13:9781539389293

DEDICATION

This is for my Mom and Dad and everyone on my planet

CONTENTS

ACKNOWLEDGMENTS

Thanks to God, Mom, Dad, Eddie, my grandparents, Jackie, my kids, my grandkids, my aunts & uncles & cousins, Father Bill, Sister Mary Vitalis, my friends & teachers from my youth (especially John Gilbert, Hector, Joe, David, Alex, Frank, Donald, Ray, Laura, Virginia, Elsa, Norma, Mrs. Copley, Mr. Cortez, and Mr. Poole), TM1 Ernie Goodman, John Kruecher, C.V. May Jr., YN1 Henderson, Felipe Cadena, Mario Borquez, Ken Buckman, Brenda, , Peaches, The Mysterious Woman, Seaman Dorsey, Doc Garrett, the crew of the USS MARVIN SHIELDS from Jan '76 to Jul '79, Chief Napasindayao, Morris Mithika Mwongo, Vladimir Pozner, Tanky Talbert, Dave Castle, Al Chiarello, Nguyen, Pak, Hong, Peggy, Mister Lee & His Magic Organ, the crew of the USS LONG BEACH from Aug '80 to Jun '83, Dee, Mike Espinola, Dennis Brown, Carol (for reasons known only to me and Mike), Wags, Pete Duta, VAQ-137 from '86-89, Rick Austin, Christine Jones, Sean Clark, Brian Annette, Tanya, Dave, Christine Fossum, ENS Gairan, Boomer, Mike Ray, The Mist, Ron "I was this close" Hardy, Roger Tapac, Safe Working Load, The Fat Bastard, Master Chief Hasse, Nando & Blackie, Lisa at Dance Home Studio, the crew of the USS CARL VINSON from Jun '93 to Jun '96, David Rodriguez, Big Al, Kat Daddy, Fred, Albert, John Villasana, Ray Symczyk, Jim Bard, Ram Ayala, , Manuela, Drumbo, Lesti Huff, Andreas & Janna Laven, El Ron of the Frozen Tundra, Gus Wanner, Kelly Hoppers, Jim Beal, Steve & Barb, Little Johnny, Lady Baker, Julianne Banks, my friends at Palo Alto College, Lee Woods, KSYM, El Rob of the Frozen Tundra, and countless others who've come into my life.

 Special thanks to Charlie Garcia, Dr. Adolfo Barrera, Susan Espinoza, Rey Valdez, Dr. Rafael Castillo, Laurie Coleman, and Juanita Luna-Lawhn who provided me with a ton of support and advice.

Quotes and Misquotes – I read a lot of stuff and wind up quoting stuff from stuff read without remembering where I read that stuff. I try to quote properly but often fail miserably. To be sure, I do like to spout off on my limited knowledge of Homer, Herodotus, Thucydides, Tacitus, Thomas Aquinas, and Patrick McManus. I sincerely apologize for anything I misquote or fail to quote due to my own faulty editing process. A big, huge thank you to James Pankow of Chicago for giving me permission to butcher his lyrics on Colour My World.

Cover photo by... me!

1 KID STUFF

When you get to be my age, you start remembering things that didn't happen and forget a lot of stuff that did happen. Fortunately, there are people with equally bad memories who've helped me piece this stuff together. The first story is forever etched in my memory and you'll understand why. "Beans" is a tale that I think everyone can relate to. "The Paddle" is absolutely 100% factual except that I changed the name of the teacher because, for the life of me, I forgot her name. "Three Barber Tales" are about my three most memorable barbershop moments. I tried to tell these stories as truthfully as possible except, I did use a little artistic license with the ending of the last barber tale.

PROBLEMS WITH MEMORY AND THE NUMBER 2

Whenever I hear people talk about their earliest memories, they usually remember things starting about age two. Everything they remember is crystal clear. I'm not one of those people. I know that, like most people, I tend to remember things I want to remember and how I want to remember them. That's why failure to pay attention to other people or one's surroundings can lead to real embarrassments.

My early conscious memories came in flashes. I vividly remember nothing. Really. Nothing. All of a sudden, someone turned on a switch in my head and I was sitting on the ground playing with my friend Tommy. I was almost four.

Women were running around screaming about possums or anteaters or skunks or something. Tommy and I went into the building we lived in to see what the screaming was all about. We looked up and saw the shadows of some kind of animals on the skylight. We thought it was funny that all the ladies were hysterical. Then the switch turned off.

The switch for my memory kept turning on and off for quite a while. I've learned that the world didn't stop when the switch was off and there was a lot of stuff that happened even before I was born. In fact, there was about twelve billion years of stuff that happened before my switch was turned on. I'll just skip all of that to say that my parents were from San Antonio, my Dad was in the Navy, my big brother Eddie was waiting for me to be born in order to inflict punishment for things I hadn't done yet, I was born in Florida when the fart assaults began, I was potty-trained in

Italy, and my Dad got transferred to Virginia when the switch turned on while we were living in Alexandria, and the women were running around screaming.

Not long after the incident with the screaming women, my Dad got word he was being transferred to the USS ALTAIRE which was home-ported in Spain. My Mom, Eddie, and I were booked on a cruise ship from New York to Barcelona. It was going to be a big adventure for us all. While in New York, I had my first real hotdog with mustard and promptly threw it up along with everything I ate for the past three months. I did not touch another hotdog or mustard for almost fifteen years and that's because I was drunk in Japan, I was hungry, and there was a corndog stand on nearly every corner in Yokosuka. But that's another story.

The switch remained on longer and longer once we arrived in Spain. The place where we lived was pretty neat. I remember that the street was cobble stone. All of the buildings were two stories tall and had balconies facing the street. The door to get in was made of wood and it was big. There was a stairway leading up and just beneath it was a little frosted glass door. Behind that door was a little white storage room that was empty except for a kerosene can and a small round tunnel that probably went off forever. I never went in there because it was dark and scary. Sometimes I'd hear spooky sounds coming out of there. Now that I think of it, it was probably just Eddie trying to scare me.

At the top of the stairs was our apartment. I remember three bedrooms, a living room, kitchen, and dining area. Eddie and I slept in the same room. Sometimes, Eddie would take off and sneak back in at night and he'd tell me about some adventures he had with his friends.

My favorite part of our place was the roof because that was where the laundry would be hung out to dry and where I would spend most of the time playing. At that time, El Cid was a popular movie around the world especially in Spain. Every kid in Spain wanted to be El Cid who liberated Valencia from the Muslims. Another hero of mine was Spartacus the gladiator who led a revolt against Rome. I was El Cid and Spartacus rolled up in one and, with my plastic sword, I killed countless Moors and Romans on that roof.

I learned there were things other than playing when I started kindergarten. I stood out immediately because I was the only American in the class. I thought it was strange that some of the kids said that I didn't look American. The other kids were very curious about my country and to my shame the only thing I could tell them about was how I played in Alexandria. Even though they were disappointed, they still treated me as a friend. In fact, the guys all gave me the number one survival tip for kindergarten. I learned the secret survival tip in a mysterious fashion. Unfortunately, I didn't know why it was important to remember it.

The bell rang and, as I was walking to class, I was suddenly surrounded by all of my male classmates. They kept pace with me and looked ahead toward the classroom.

"Pssst!"

I turned to look at the kid walking to my right and immediately felt a pinch on my left arm.

"Don't look! She's watching!" whispered one kid.

"Who?"

"The teacher, estupido!" said another kid.

The kid to my right then said, "Listen carefully! If you have to go the bathroom, the teacher's going to ask you if you have to do Number One or Number Two. "

"Always tell her you have to do Number One," said the kid to my left.

Then from behind me, another kid piped in, "Always say, Number One even if you have to do Number Two!"

The kid to my right finished by saying, "If you do have to do Number Two, you better do it fast!"

"But why?"

I got no reply since we were in class and had to take our seats. Over the next few days, I noticed that every time a boy raised his hand to go to the bathroom, Senorita Garza (our beautiful, yet mildly sadistic teacher) would ask whether he had to go Number One or Number Two. The answer would invariably be "Number One, Senorita Garza!" She would let the kid go and continue with the class while looking at the clock. Every kid would return to class quickly. I noticed that a couple of them would be out of breath.

I remember the first time a kid took more than five minutes to get back to class. He had told Senorita Garza that he had to do Number One. He ran out of the class and clock started ticking. Our teacher kept looking at the clock and after five minutes, she went to the door and walked down the hall.

"Oh, no!" someone whispered. "He's taking too long!"

Soon, we could hear the teacher's high heels clicking up the hall as well as the shuffling of a pair of oxfords. Miss Garza held the kid by the ear. He was obviously very embarrassed, and his face turned red as all of the guys said, "oooooo" in unison. She gave him three whacks of the paddle, told him she was going to tell his parents that he was a liar, and sent him to his seat.

I didn't understand why he would've lied about doing Number One instead of Number Two if he was going to get paddled. None of the guys would tell me. They just shook their heads and patted him on the back. Then they all laughed at him and told him he'd better learn to squeeze it out faster.

There were several times that I had to go to the bathroom while in class. I'd raise my hand, get asked if I was doing Number One or Number Two and I would always say, "Number One." I always said, "Number One" because it was the truth. So, the days flew by with everyone always doing Number One and getting back to class on time. I had forgotten about the warning and the lesson of the kid who took too long.

One day, I really had to go the bathroom bad. I raised my hand and when I was asked what I had to do, I truthfully answered, "Number Two." There were gasps throughout the room. My friends gasped. The girls gasped. Even the kids who didn't like me gasped. My friend, Pedrito, slapped his forehead and hissed, "Estupido!" I didn't know what everyone was so upset about. I walked out of the class and into the bathroom.

I covered the toilet seat with toilet paper just as Mom taught me to do whenever sitting on a strange toilet. I sat down and pooped. It didn't take long. I cleaned myself and checked the paper every wipe until there was no mark on it to make sure I was clean. I flushed the toilet, opened the stall door, and there was Senorita Garza waiting for me with a roll of toilet paper in hand.

"Gilberto, take off your pants. I have to check you to make sure you're clean."

"But, Senorita," I said. "I cleaned myself real good just like my mother taught me."

The teacher would have none of it. She explained to me that as a teacher, it was her responsibility not only to teach, but to send kids back to their parents as clean as when they came to school, after all, she continued, "what would your parents think if I sent you home with caca on your underwear?" She proceeded to place two squares of toilet paper on her middle finger, grabbed me by the neck, bent me over and wiped my butt once with that paper wrapped finger. She had sharp finger nails.

She looked at the paper and said sweetly, "You did a very good job of cleaning yourself, Gilberto. Now go wash your hands."

As I walked in the classroom with Senorita Garza, I heard "oooooo" and then I understood the warning my classmates gave me. Oh, the humanity! As I slowly walked back to my desk, I could hear the snickering of my friends. They all knew what had happened. Oh, the shame of it all. Recess was going to be hell.

I went out to the playground and found a corner to hide in, so I wouldn't get harassed. My world had just crumbled into ruins. No kid in the history of school ever had their butt wiped by the teacher and not have every kid in class find out about it. No one would ever be my friend. I was marked for life.

"Hey, Idiota!"

I looked up and saw Pedrito walking toward me with several other guys. Well, this is it, I thought. I prepared myself for the worst. I lowered my head as the guys surrounded me. I felt an arm around my shoulders. It was Pedrito and he was smiling.

"Estupido, didn't we tell you to never say you were doing Number Two?" my friend asked.

"Huh?"

Tino cut in, "She always wipes your butt if you do Number Two!"

"Yeah, all of us got it," said Pedrito, "Miguel got caught three times!"

Miguel nodded and said, "She needs to cut her fingernails."

"Her middle finger was really sharp," I said.

We all laughed. I didn't feel so bad anymore because, after all, every one of us had been wiped by Senorita Garza. From that moment, I became one of the guys and I made sure my memory switch stayed on after that.

BEANS

I really liked spending weekends with my grandparents. My Abuelita was a very short, dark, slightly rounded woman with a beaming smile and very long hair which she braided and tied in a bun. She could cook like nobody's business. Living in a region where beans are a staple of everyone's diet can give people a discriminating taste when it comes to beans. Her beans were the best. I have yet to find any beans that compared to the beans of my youth.

Abuelito was about a foot taller than my grandmother. He had dark, weathered skin and his hands were calloused from working as a carpenter. He had straight, fine hair which was always slicked back. He had a big nose. He smoked Lucky Strikes, drank Lone Star, and lived for All Star Wrestling.

Abuelita always made her tortillas from scratch. I liked to watch her as she would pat the masa between her hands. It sounded like a quiet applause. Sometimes she would sing or sometimes she'd tell stories while making the tortillas. Of course, she never made tortillas without making rice and beans so the kitchen smelled wonderful. Once she finished the first batch of tortillas, she would call the men to the table. She wouldn't eat until everyone had their fill.

I remember that the only knife on the table was where Abuelito sat because he was the one who cut anything that needed cutting like the green onions that we put on the beans. The centerpiece of the table was a bowl of salt from which we would grab a pinch to season our food. Although forks were placed by our plates, no one ever used them because we all followed the example of my grandfather who would tear his tortilla into four equal pieces and use them to scoop up his food.

One time while we were eating, I yelled out, "These beans are the best!" Abuelita who was making another batch of tortillas said, "Ai, thank you, Mijo!" Abuelito laughed and said, "You got that right! That's why I married your abuela."

"Payaso!" my grandmother hissed as she swatted him with a dish cloth.

He continued, "All of the women used to chase me because I was so handsome. But I did not care for them because they did not know how to cook. I promised myself that I would only marry the woman who made the best beans in the world, so I went on a long journey to find those beans.

"One day, I was walking down the street and I smelled beans. I followed my nose to that wonderful smell and there was your abuelita cooking her beans," he said. He scooped up some beans with a piece of tortilla and said, "I tasted her beans." Abuelito then stuffed his mouth with the beans and with that full mouth he said, "Those beans were the best in the entire world. I told her that she had to marry me and she could not refuse me because I was so handsome!"

"Curioso!" Abuelita exclaimed as she swatted him with the dish cloth. My grandfather seemed to get hit with the dish cloth a lot.

One day we were having lunch and Abuelito was strangely quiet. He chopped a couple of green onions and dropped some on my beans. Abuelita left the kitchen to get something from the front of the house. Abuelito tore a tortilla into four sections. He hunched over his beans with his left arm on the table almost cradling the beans. His right hand held a piece of tortilla. He looked around to check that my grandmother was not around. He then leaned forward and looked me square in the eye. He had the look of someone about to reveal something very serious. And then he spoke.

"Mijo, do you know why it's good to be Mexican?"

"No, Abuelito. Why?"

My grandfather squinted both of his eyes. He slowly looked to his left. He slowly looked to his right. He scooped up some beans with a piece of tortilla and as he shoved the beans into his mouth he exclaimed, "Because we can eat our spoons!"

The dish cloth came flying out of nowhere.

THE PADDLE

Brentwood Elementary School was a great school. I loved it. I was in the third grade and I was in love with Miss Espinoza. It was the spring of 1965 and all sorts of stuff was in the air. Sure, there were pretty girls in class like Sandra, Sarah, and Laura but girls my age just seemed to smell funny and none of them had legs like my substitute teacher, Miss Espinoza.

Speaking of legs, I love legs. Always have. My favorite legs were the ones that were attached to Miss Flores. She was a dance instructor. She was beautiful, and I loved looking at her. But looking at her came with a price. I had to take dance lessons and I hated it. My Mom wanted me to learn Mexican folk dance. Lucky for me my agony was shared by my friend, Hector. His Mom made him take lessons too. We had to wear little charro outfits with sombreros and all of the ladies our parents knew would say how cute we looked and tell their sons how they should be more like Hector and Gilbert and we were pretty embarrassed except during dance class because there were piles of pretty girls all over the place.

There were times when Hector and I didn't have to dance with our partners, so we would slip out behind the dance studio and throw rocks in the drainage ditch. I remember we got in trouble once when our moms found us in the ditch. After that, we had to stay inside and watch the girls dance. I don't know how he did it but, Hector convinced his mom to let him quit so I was stuck alone.

I took up drawing during the lulls in rehearsals. I thought I was pretty good; well as good as a third grader could be. I took to drawing super heroes. I drew Spider Man, Super Man, and Thor. I also created my own super heroes. One of them was Carbon Man. He shot out black stuff from his fists and turned villains into charcoal. I started drawing all the time, even in school.

The school I went to was Brentwood Elementary. It was located on the Westside of San Antonio close to Kelly AFB. It was unique in the fact that it had a diverse population. Back then, schools were somewhat segregated by race. I don't think it was intentional because San Antonio was pretty much divided into three distinct districts: The Anglos in the North, the Blacks in the East, and the Mexicans in the West and South. My neighborhood was different because the Kelly and Lackland Air Force bases were there. We were pretty mixed, but we were still mainly a Mexican school.

In those days, darned near every teacher was a White lady with a ruler. They were generally pretty nice except whenever we mixed up a ch with an sh and vice versa. "No, Lucy! It's not 'SHicken,' it's 'Chicken!'" they would scream. Even if a kid caught someone doing something wrong and told the teacher, they'd get in trouble. "Ma'am! Hector is sheating!" The ruler would come out with a whack! "No! It's 'Cheating' not 'Sheating!'"

Having gone through first grade in DC, I didn't understand why so many of my friends had problems pronouncing words that started with ch or sh. I think we went through every year in elementary repeating the same exercise to correct the problem. "All right, class, repeat after me: Share the chair with the sheet on the child."

"Chare the shair with the cheet on the shild." And so, it went year after year.

I still remember when we got a Mexican substitute teacher for the first time. Miss Espinoza was the most beautiful creature to walk the planet Earth. She had brown skin. It wasn't a dark brown like people I knew who worked outside in the sun. It was a soft, light brown like that of someone who spent time in the shade reading poetry, going to museums, and occasionally picking flowers on a nice day. She had a face like an angel, kind and infinitely good like La Virgen de Guadalupe only younger and prettier. She wore red lipstick and the warmth of her smile could melt the coldest of hearts. Her eyes were a dark brown, almost black, with long luscious eyelashes. Her hair was black as night and shiny. She was slender, not busty, and she wore tight skirts that came just above her beautiful knees. Her black high heels accentuated what I swear to this day were the most artistically perfect legs that ever existed. Her voice was sweet and tender. I heard music every time she spoke.

I was in love.

I remember that she cried a lot. That was because some of my classmates didn't seem to love her the way I did. A bunch of my friends seemed to get a kick out of making her cry. Whenever she started crying, she would run out of class and the culprit would be called in to see Mrs. Hoelsher our principal.

Now Mrs. Hoelsher was almost the opposite of Miss Espinoza in the way of looks. She was old. She was White. She was thick. She had thick legs and wore big, thick black shoes with thick heels that made a "clump, clump" sound down the hall whenever she was about. She had grey hair. I never thought she was ugly because she had a kindly face. She had big, thick arms and, for some reason, every kid in school was terrified of her. There were stories told about her paddle and kids who were sent to her office came out maimed for life. If a kid went in twice, he was never seen again.

Well, I had no desire to make Miss Espinoza cry. Not me. I wanted her to smile. I wanted her to smile at me and I did everything I could to make her happy. I was always on time. I did my homework and I always tried to do something nice for her. I was her favorite student. She always drew a little smiling face next to the grade I received on my work.

I was a pretty good student back then. I always got high scores and finished my work before everyone else. This meant that I had extra time to fool around. I used that time to draw pictures for Miss Espinoza whenever she subbed. She really liked them. Now since I was a kid, I didn't always draw butterflies and flowers. That would've been weird. I took to creating short comic books of my invented heroes.

My buddies liked my comics, so I started selling them for a nickel apiece. I had a pretty brisk business going. Miss Espinoza sometimes caught me drawing but I never got in trouble since I always did my work first.

One day a friend of mine named Ricky, who bought a few of my comics, came up with an idea for me to make more money. He told me that I could make more money if I started drawing girls in bikinis and high heels. He told me that I could probably get a quarter for each picture. He would help me sell them if he would ten cents for each one and I would get fifteen. Well, that seemed to be a good idea to me at the time. The only problem was I didn't know what a girl in a bikini looked like.

The only model I had for a beautiful girl was Miss Espinoza. I had done dozens of pictures of my love holding flowers or butterflies or birds. I gave every one of them to her. Every time I drew a girl it was always with the same face; the face of Miss Espinoza. I remember seeing the Annett Funicello movies and was particularly taken with Connie Stevens who wore a bikini. That gave me the vision of how to draw a girl in a bikini. My big problem was that the only beautiful face I could draw was that of Miss Espinoza, so my bikini girl had the body of Connie Stevens with the head of Miss Espinoza.

Ricky was selling my drawings like hotcakes. I think I made almost two dollars when Miss Espinoza came up to my desk while I was drawing. I was working on a master piece. I had the profile perfect. Connie Stevens' body was sitting on the beach, wearing high heels, leaning back with arms behind holding her up and Miss Espinoza's head tilted back looking at the seagulls.

"Oh, Gilbert," she said, "what a…"

She gasped.

I looked up at her and saw tears welling up in her beautiful eyes.

She ran out of the classroom.

Oh, no! I laid my head on my desk. I was mortified. I just made Miss Espinoza cry. I felt terrible. I made Miss Espinoza cry. I made the woman I love cry!

After what seemed like an eternity I heard the "clomp, clomp, clomp" of Mrs. Hoelscher's shoes coming straight to the classroom. Every kid in the room was as quiet as a mouse. Every kid in the room looked straight at me with the "ooh, you're in some big trouble now" look. I think I remember my friend, Albert, saying, "She's gonna kill him!"

The door opened.

"Gilbert Polanco?"

I stood up. My head was down.

I followed Mrs. Hoelscher down the hall. The walk of shame seemed to take years. When we got to her office, she said in a sad voice, "Please sit down, Gilbert." I sat down on the chair in front of her desk. I held my head low, not wanting to look at her.

"Look at me, Gilbert."

I looked up trying my best not to cry.

I expected Mrs. Hoelscher to be angry and snarling. I expected her to bite my head off. I wish she had. Instead, her face was sad. It looked almost as if she wanted to cry. She looked hurt and that was much worse than facing an angry principal.

"I'm disappointed in you," she said in a soft, sad voice. "You've always been such a good student. I know that Miss Espinoza thinks the world of you. I just don't understand how you could've done such a horrible thing. Did someone put you up to this?"

I may have been the lowest form of life on Earth, but I wasn't a rat. I didn't tell her it was Ricky's idea. Well, that's the way I remember it. Come to think of it, I was pretty much a lambiache back then. Yep, I was a real kiss ass, so I probably did rat him out.

Mrs. Hoelscher then gave me *the talk*. Most of it had to do with respect for women. Every woman is somebody's sister, daughter, or mother and deserving of respect. How would I feel if someone mistreated my mom or one of my friend's sisters? Miss Espinoza was a kind and caring teacher who really like me a lot. I had broken her trust and broke her heart as well.

"I'm sorry! I'm sorry!" I cried. Boy, did I cry. I think my tears could've filled the janitor's bucket.

"I know you're sorry, Gilbert," she replied, "but being sorry isn't good enough. What you did was bad, and you have to learn that there are consequences for your actions."

I looked at The Paddle hanging on the wall behind her desk. It was the first time I ever saw The Paddle. I heard my friends speak of it in whispers. It was always described as an instrument of Doom. It was a little more than a foot long, about half as wide, and an inch thick. The handle was wrapped with athletic tape and there were holes drilled into the business end. I was told that it could rip the flesh off your butt with one whack. There wasn't any old flesh hanging from it and I didn't see any bloodstains on it. Perhaps she cleaned it after every execution.

"What you did needs to be punished. Normally, I would call your parents and let them deal with you."

Oh, no. Dad would kill me and that was okay, but Mom…

"However," she continued, "I know your mother. She is a very nice woman. I know that if she found out about this it would just break her heart. I don't want to do that. You've always been a good student and since this is your first offense I'm going to let you decide what I should do. I can suspend you for the rest of the day and have your mother pick you up or you can get paddled."

I could see the shock and hurt in my mother's eyes. She would be ashamed of me. I didn't want to ever make her cry. Anything would be better than making my Mom cry. There was no other choice.

"I'll take The Paddle, Ma'am," I whispered.

"Very well, Gilbert. Please stand up."

I stood up and placed my hands on her desk. Mrs. Hoelscher stood up slowly and reached for The Paddle. She walked up behind me. I steadied myself. I knew I would never be able to walk again.

"Gilbert, it hurts me to have to do this. You are the last boy I ever thought I would have to paddle."

It seemed to take forever for her to wind up to administer the death blow. The silence was deafening. I heard her sigh and then there was a whack. It wasn't a WHACK! It was just a whack. I didn't feel my bones break. I didn't feel the flesh ripped from my butt. It was just a whack. Just one whack.

I waited for another whack, but it didn't come. I stood up straight and looked at Mrs. Hoelscher. There were tears in her eyes. I don't know what came over me but, I ran and threw my arms around her and bawled like a baby.

"I'm sorry!" I cried. "I'm so sorry!"

She held me tenderly and patted my head. "I know. I know," she said. "You should tell Miss Espinoza how you feel. Now please go back to class and promise me that you won't do anything like this again."

"I promise, Ma'am."

I went to the restroom and washed my face. I then ran to Miss Espinoza's class to apologize. All eyes were on my when I entered the room. Every guy was looking to see if I had any broken bones. Every girl gave me a dirty look and seemed disappointed that I didn't have any broken bones. Miss Espinoza was gone. In her place was Mrs. Klausner who was filling in because Miss Espinoza had taken ill.

I didn't get into trouble again until the fifth grade when I hit Sylvia Ayala with a rock. That's a whole other story though.

I need to mention that Mrs. Hoelscher remained at Brentwood Elementary for many years. She was loved and respected by everyone who knew her. Yeah, there were some kids who were scared to death of her, but I knew better. She was a wise principal who really cared for her students. She took her job seriously because she knew that her responsibility was not to be a babysitter. She was an educator dedicated to the education and molding of children in to good citizens. She died a few years back and Brentwood was renamed Hoelscher Elementary School in honor of this wonderful woman.

As for Miss Espinoza, I wrote her a long letter apologizing for what I did. I even gave her a flower. She accepted my apology in a very gracious manner. I made sure that I did everything I could to make her happy whenever she subbed. I got 100's on all of my work and everything went back to normal, except for one thing:

I never saw a smiley face on my papers ever again.

THREE BARBER TALES

My mom used to fix my hair when I was little, and I didn't like it at all. There's something about how moms fix the hair of their sons while saying things like, "Ai, Mijo! You look so handsome!" that make those same sons ashamed to be seen in public. It's not so bad when you're really little, but when you reach the ripe old age of seven it can be torture. The only thing worse is having your mom kiss you good-bye when she drops you off in front of Brentwood Elementary School. Talk about a death sentence. It is right then that a boy starts wishing he wasn't little. So, the first grownup experience is a milestone in a kid's life. I remember mine vividly.

The Rocket Barbershop was an icon of Cupples Road in San Antonio back in the Sixties. La Sirena Lounge, The Arrow Ice House (which everyone knew as Coke's), Ed's Inn, Benavidez Food Mart, The Taco House, Chino's, and the O&R Lounge could also be considered icons. There was another icon smack dab next to The Rocket that was mentioned in whispers: Bernie's Flower Shop. Bernie was what grownups would refer to as "flamboyant." I didn't know what "flamboyant" meant but I heard my parents refer to Liberace as "flamboyant" and I figured it meant that Bernie talked and acted funny. Thankfully, my first grownup experience had nothing to do with Bernie. The first time I felt like a big kid was in The Rocket Barbershop.

I had been to The Rocket many times with my mother who got tired of cutting my hair and cleaning up the mess. I really hated going there because she would make me dress up like I was going to visit relatives, pack me in her white 1963 Valiant and drive to the end of the block where she would park, get out, admire the floral arrangements at Bernie's, and then drag me inside the barbershop. I always held my head down in shame, so I never really noticed my surroundings.

The barbers would greet my Mom, "Mrs. Polanco! How can we help you?" She would respond in a sweet voice, "Mijo's here for a haircut." When she was asked what type of haircut I should get, she'd invariably order the "Little Boys Haircut." She continually gave directions to the barber during the entire ordeal. When the barber was finished, Mom would get a comb from her purse and fix my hair, so it was perfect. Then the barber would hold out an open jar of lollypops, so I could grab one. I'd reach in without bothering to look, grab the first lollypop, say "thank you" and try to run out as fast as possible but Mom was faster and was able to grab my hand even as she paid the barber.

Did the torture stop with leaving the barbershop? Oh, no! My Mom, my loving mother, just had to take me somewhere she could show me off. Sometimes we'd visit relatives. Sometimes we'd go to Shopper's World. Sometimes we'd go downtown to The New Mexican Manhattan next to the Solo Serv to eat.

On a side note, I always wondered if there ever was an Old Mexican Manhattan because more than fifty years later, one can still eat at the New Mexican Manhattan. Either way, no matter where we went, there was always some old lady pinching my cheeks or patting my head telling Mom what a good-looking son she had, and I would suck on the stupid lollypop which was always lime or pineapple (I hated both) and never cherry or grape (which I liked) because concentrating on the disgusting taste at least distracted me a little from the humiliation being heaped on me. So, it's no wonder I hated Haircut Day.

One Saturday, before my ninth birthday, Mom told me to get dressed so I could get a haircut. I closed my eyes and walked to my room to get my clothes. I knew there was no way out and I was resigned to endure what was to come. And then a superhero came to my rescue.

"Hey, Lupe, I'll take Gil to get his haircut," my Dad said, "and we'll pick up some burgers from Coke's on our way back." I never had a haircut without my Mom being present. I started to change but Dad told me I could go just as I was. Wow! I didn't have to change! I didn't even have to wash up! Mom stopped us just as we were walking out the door and cleaned my ears inside and out with a wet wash cloth. While I was getting my ears cleaned, Dad took advantage of the diversion and grabbed a cold Falstaff beer from the fridge. "Come on. Let's go," he said.

As we left the yard, Mom called out, "Gilbert! Hold your father's hand!" Dad just turned around and said, "Lupe, he's old enough to walk on his own." My hero! I couldn't believe my good fortune! He then gave me a five-dollar bill and told me that I should give the barber a fifty-cent tip after I paid for the haircut. Oh boy, this was great! It only got better when he handed me the unopened beer and said, "Here, hold this for a minute." He reached in his shirt pocket, pulled out a King Edward cigar and lit it with his Zippo.

I started to see Dad in a different light. He wasn't around much during my first six years on Earth because he was in the Navy and at sea a lot until he retired when I was six. When I did see him, he was a funny guy who liked to strike goofy poses whenever he farted. On Saturdays, he'd make me pancakes in the shape of different animals.

Dad had straight, fine, black hair that was always cut close to the sides. He was short and dark skinned with strong Mexican-Indian features. He liked beer and developed a bit of a gut when he retired. He laughed a lot. He was a darned good father but that day he went from being my dad to being my Dad.

We walked up to The Rocket which was in a small, single story cinder block building that it shared with Bernie's Flower Shop. It was painted green and white like the John F. Kennedy High School Mighty Rockets football jerseys. Situated just off the corner, the building shared the side of the block with an empty lot that was being cleared for the construction of an apartment building. The parking lot was all gravel and dust which got all over my shoes. Mom would get mad at Dad about that later.

The door to The Rocket had a bell attached to it that jingled every time it was opened. As we walked in, the two barbers (for the life of me, I can't remember their names) who were sitting in the barber chairs reading the paper and this old guy who always seemed to be there stood up and greeted us with a "Hey, come on in!" They started making with the small talk. I stood there and just smelled the air. I liked the way it smelled. The aroma of Clubman, Tres Flores, witch hazel, Aqua Velva, hair wax, lilac water, Brylcreem, and Barbicide disinfectant mixed with the odors of smoke and beer made the place feel like this is a man's hangout. For some reason, it never felt like that when I came with my Mom.

Just as I was getting lost in the smells of The Rocket, one of the barbers looked at me and asked, "Well, Mister Polanco, what can I do for you today?"

Wow! He called me Mister Polanco! I told him I needed a haircut and he responded, "Take a seat, Sir!" as he placed the big kids' booster seat on the barber chair. I'd always had my haircut while sitting on the little kids' booster so, at that moment, I was really feeling good.

"And what kind of cut would you like, Sir?" asked the barber.

I looked to my Dad for guidance, but he was busy reading a Dapper magazine. I should mention that before arrival of feminism and the "sensitivity" that's been forced on every nearly extinct refuge of real men, girly magazines such as Gent and Dapper were required reading in every barbershop throughout this great country. Every barbershop, garage, gas station, and lumber company also had a girly calendar on display for all to see. I always wondered why either a barber or customer would toss a towel on top of the end table every time my Mom opened the door. This time there was no towel on the table and the magazine covers were clearly visible. So, I learned the unwritten rule that whoever was near the table had the duty of covering the magazines with a towel whenever a woman entered the barbershop.

Even though I was fascinated by the lurid magazine covers, the fact that the barber had asked me what kind of haircut I would like left me all sorts of excited. I looked at the sign on the wall directly in front of me that listed the types and prices of the haircuts I could choose. The list wasn't all that long. I had the choice of the Styled, Regular, Crew Cut, Flat Top, Trim, and the dreaded Little Boys Cut.

"I'll take the Regular!"

I guess I shouted it out a little too loudly because the men in the barbershop all chuckled except for the barber who said, "That's a good choice." He then wrapped a thin sheet of paper, kind of like wax paper without the wax, around my neck and clipped it with something that looked like a money clip. He then clipped the cutting cloth on me and adjusted the height of the chair using his foot on a lever at the chair's base.

As the barber cut my hair, I was aware that the men were talking about all sorts of things I didn't quite understand. There was talk about the Longhorns and politics and stuff I really didn't care about. The topic that did catch my attention was when talk turned to NASA and the Gemini missions. I don't think there was a kid in the country who didn't know something about space exploration. I knew that Ed White was commanding the next flight because it was in my Weekly Reader.

The barber snapped me out of my daydreams of space flight when he asked me if I wanted the back of my neck blocked or tapered. I thought of asking if he could give it a duckbill the way some of the older kids were wearing their hair, but I quickly envisioned my Mom yelling at my Dad about how her little boy looks like a pachuco. I went with the block cut.

I knew it was nearly time to get out of the chair when the barber started brushing the hair off my ears, neck, and shoulders. Soon afterwards, he would ask my Dad how he liked my hair, my hair would get combed, the cutting cloth would come off, I'd get a lollypop and it would be over. But I was wrong. Instead of my chair going down, I heard a pfffffft sound behind me and then felt hot lather being spread around my ears and the back of my neck. A small towel was placed on my left shoulder. The barber then pulled out a straight razor and ran it back and forth across the shaving strop.

"Hold still."

I held still.

I felt a big hand tilt my head toward my right shoulder. I felt a finger just above my temple keeping my head in place while a thumb held my left ear down. Then I felt the razor scraping against the skin behind my ear. After every third scrape, I could feel the razor being wiped clean of lather on the towel that was on my shoulder. My head was then tilted forward, and the back of my neck was shaved. The process was then repeated on the right side of my head.

The barber cleaned behind my ears and neck with a warm wash cloth, splashed some Florida Water on his hands, patted my face and rubbed my neck and the back of my ears in what seemed like one smooth motion. I was then spun around to face the large mirror on the wall while the barber held a smaller mirror behind my head, so I could admire his handy work. He then handed me a comb to style my hair as I saw fit. With a final brushing of hair off my shoulders, the chair was lowered, and I followed the barber to the cash register. He turned to me and asked, "Will there be anything else, Sir?"

Since I'd never been asked that question and it was the first time that I was the actual customer, I looked around to see if there was anything else. Hanging right next to the girly calendar was a cardboard display and stapled to it were plastic pocket brushes. Having a pocket brush was like having a sign that says, "I'm cool" because all you did was slip it on your finger and two swipes of your head left your hair neatly in place. Of course, you needed a toothpick hanging from your lip to really look cool.

The barber handed me my brand spanking new pocket brush and said, "That'll be two-fifty, Sir." I nonchalantly handed him the five-dollar bill. He gave me two-fifty in change and I, in turn, handed him two quarters and told him, "Here's for your trouble."

Dad and I left The Rocket and walked over to Coke's. I pulled out the two dollars change to give to him, but he told me to keep it and buy what I wanted. I ordered a burger and fries and a Hippo Red. I paid Coke a dollar and walked back home with my Dad feeling a little bit taller.

- - -

Over the next four years, I learned that men who hung around barbershops were knowledgeable or experienced in everything from skipping stones to rocket science. I also learned that what at first seemed to be a pack of lies turned out to contain big, fat Kernels of Truth. I was really learning the ropes from those guys at The Rocket but, when I turned thirteen I started listening to that evil Rock-N-Roll which, for some mysterious reason, caused my hair to recoil from the sight of a barber's pole. I didn't sit in a barber's chair again until my first day in Navy boot camp. Let me tell you, it was nothing like The Rocket.

I really don't remember much about that day except for there was a lot of screaming and spit was flying everywhere. The company commanders had the ability curse with such power their saliva would be expelled by the sheer force of the curse and fly ahead to splatter a cowering recruit before the verbal shock wave arrived, cracking at least three teeth.

I remember standing in line at the barbershop, watching long haired rockers walk in and weeping bald kids shuffling out. As I stepped inside, I saw a line of eight barber chairs and seated on them were eight frightened recruits. Hovering above them were eight crazed Navy barbers, their eyes and shears gleaming with maniacal glee. The eight maniacs seemed to ask simultaneously in a very pleasant yet darkly evil tone, "How would you like your haircut, Sir?" Just as the recruits relaxed enough to say, "Well, I, uh…" the barbers pounced on their hapless victims.

BZZZZZZZZ!!!!!!!

Yaaaaaaaah!!!!!

Mommy!!!!!!

Oh, the screams were incredible.

As the weeping recruits shuffled by me, I looked to see if there were any earlobes missing. I didn't see any missing, but I couldn't be sure since I could only see one side of their heads. As I walked toward the Barber Chair of Doom, I looked down to see if any earlobes were on the ground. There were none, but then again, the barbers were constantly sweeping the deck.

I walked up to the chair and noticed my barber. He seemed to be a kindly sort of fellow. He looked to be the type that you could hang out with in a sports bar. He smiled. It was a friendly smile. He didn't seem evil at all. He seemed nice. He whispered to me, "Don't them scare you. My buddies are a bunch of assholes." I relaxed. I was lucky to get the nice barber.

He put his hand on my left shoulder and asked in a pleasant voice, "How would you like your haircut, Sir?"

I turned to him and said, "Well, I, uh…" and then he pounced.

BZZZZZZZZ!!!!!!!

Yaaaaaaaah!!!!!

Mommy!!!!!!

Oh, the screams were incredible.

- - -

During the twenty years I spent in the Navy, I got my haircuts exclusively from Navy barbers. The only break in that routine was during a four-year shore tour in Minneapolis. It turned out that there was no real base there like I was used to in the past. There were no military barbers to speak of nearby, so I looked for a civilian barbershop.

I happened upon Rollie's Barbershop while exploring the area near the Reserve Center. It was a week before I had to report for duty and three weeks since I had a haircut. I hoped this barber knew how to give a proper military haircut. You see, barbers are a dying breed. They're nearly extinct and you can thank those pro-clip, hair crafty, pretentious corporate hair styling chop shops that hire unenthusiastic butchers who couldn't give a crew cut to save their mothers' souls.

I stepped into Rollie's and the smell of that place transported me back to my childhood and the joy that was The Rocket. The smells were all there from the hair tonic to the Barbicide. Of course, with the advent of the modern "enlightened" society, there was no cigar smoke nor was there the smell of stale whiskey. The magazines were different as was the calendar. Girls were replaced by pictures of moose, fly fishermen, and The Vikings.

It didn't matter. Rollie's was a real barbershop!

Now Rollie was a big, Nordic kind of guy. He knew how to cut hair. In fact, I think that he was one of the best barbers I ever met which is why I didn't understand why there was no shortage of Rollie haircut jokes being told by the customers. One example of a Rollie joke was told by an older gentleman who had just had his hair cut and was just hanging around. He was looking in the mirror and brushed off a few hair clippings from his shoulders when he said, "Yuh know I just got back from London. Rollie's mighty famous there, don'tcha know?"

I bit the hook and said, "Really? I didn't know that."

"Ya, yuh betcha! I wuz walking by this hatter's place there and the owner steps oot, hands me a hat and he sez to me he sez, 'Put this on, ye poor chap! I see that Rollie's got 'is hands on ye!"

Everyone laughed except Rollie and the guy who was getting his haircut. Rollie simply smiled and said, "You're lucky you told that joke after I cut your hair."

I must have looked concerned for the man because the old guy turned to me and said, "Rollie's got a short memory. Besides, he's done permanently damaged my head already. Just don't be like that kid that walked in last year wearing the hat that said, 'THIS HAT IS COVERING A HAIRCUT FROM ROLLIES.'"

"What happened to him?"

"That young man no longer requires haircuts or even solid food."

I learned that Rollie's customers were quite loyal and they didn't seem to suffer too much. I came to believe that maybe they were just being friendly and stretching the truth regarding Rollie's fame because every time I went to get a haircut, the stories got wilder.

I really missed Rollie's when I left Minnesota and when I returned for a visit a couple of years later, I went straight to that barbershop. Rollie actually recognized me. I sat in the familiar barber chair and listened to a Rollie joke while Rollie threatened the comedian.

As Rollie placed the cutting cloth around my neck, he said, "Son, it looks like you haven't had a haircut since the last time you were here."

I nonchalantly replied, "That's right Rollie. Ever since you last cut my hair, I swore that no man would ever touch my head again."

Needless to say, the screams were incredible.

2 UNHEALTHY STUFF

The following two stories are absolutely true. They both take place about two months apart. I was about 50 at the time and having a blast playing drums with several bands. Up to that point, my only doctor visits were for check-ups, shots, and the occasional stitch or forty-two (that's another story). I had survived many scrapes and considered myself pretty, darned lucky. Well, my luck took a freaky turn because my first actual hospitalization since birth happened to be followed by my second hospitalization two months later. The stories are funny now, but I wasn't laughing when they happened.

THE BIG TRIP

It seems to me that my life can never be simple. The strangest things happen to me, I kid you not. Maybe it's because I've traveled so much that I've experienced both interesting and frightening things my entire life. A good example of an interesting and frightening experience that's almost unbelievable even without embellishment happened to me about three years ago.

It had been awhile since I'd taken a long vacation and I really needed some rest. To me, rest and relaxation is hitting the road to see friends or family and I wanted to do both. My friends, Shawn and Brian, lived in Minnesota and my son was visiting my daughter who was living in Washington State. I figured that I could take about three weeks and drive from San Antonio to Minneapolis then Washington and back to SA in no time. I planned every part of the trip except for the parts I didn't plan.

I called Shawn to ask about the weather and I learned that due to the sun getting hotter, Minnesota had seen little or no snow. I did a little research and found that even the polar caps on Mars were melting. Now that's some greenhouse gas don'tcha know! It was Spring Break, so it came as a shock when I saw snow falling as I hit the Twin Cities. In fact, I saw a freakin' snow storm!

I had planned to stay about four or five days and jam with my friends. We wound up in the basement studio that belonged to El Rob of the Frozen Tundra. Since Brian couldn't make it the first day, Shawn and I recorded my country song "What the F**k Are You Doing to Me" with El Rob on bass and rhythm which happens to be on my website. The next night, Brian showed up and we recorded some of our jams including "La Sirena Lounge" and proceeded to get all sorts of messed up.

Meanwhile, it kept snowing and I was worried about getting stuck. The forecast was for more snow, so it was with some relief that I heard there was going to be a break in the snowfall on the third day of my visit. I decided to hightail it out of there while I had the chance. In my feeble mind, I hoped to make it to Billings, Montana in between blizzards.

I woke up with a slight hangover and jumped into my Ford Escape. After grabbing a coffee and donut, I headed west on Interstate 94 praying that I'd have clear weather the whole day. I was pretty much relieved when I saw a clear, blue sky. There was a slight chill in the air, but it looked like clear sailing for me. That is, until I passed Fargo. There, in front of me, on the road, the very road on which I was driving was a light powdery snow wisping across the road like the mist atop a bowl of dry ice blown by a handheld fan. I've been up North enough to know that when one sees a light, powdery snow sort of wisping across a road like the mist atop a bowl of dry ice blown by a handheld fan, one should not hang around to admire the gentle beauty of the scene but rather seek immediate shelter.

There was no shelter. The blizzard was coming. I wasn't going to reach Billings that day. I wasn't sure I would reach any place but Doom because there didn't seem to be any town in that desolate land. I was getting scared because the snow was coming down faster and the wind was blowing harder and I could barely make out a straight gray line leading into the blinding white of Oblivion.

Approximately 20 miles from the Middle of Nowhere, I saw a sign for a town named Beach. The snowfall lightened up a bit, so I could survey the area. I turned right off 95 and saw a gas station to my left. There was a small road leading to a white motel building about a quarter mile down. I looked to my right and, down that road, there was another motel.

That motel gave me the creeps. It seemed dirty. The windows looked to be blacked out and there was only one only pickup truck parked in the lot. I looked to my left and noticed that there were several cars parked at the white motel. I thought to myself, *do I stay at the white motel that has people staying there or do I stay at the deserted, Evil Motel?* I decided against the evil motel and drove to the white one. For the life of me, I can't remember the name of that motel.

Pulling into the parking lot, I noticed that there was no shelter for the cars and most of them were parked along the outer wall of the motel for protection from the wind. I found a spot near the entrance and parked. I walked inside and started getting *The Creeps*.

Upon entering, I saw a half-flight of stairs leading down to the motel rooms in a dark hallway and another half-flight of stairs leading up to more rooms in another dark hallway. To my immediate left was a small, dimly lit lounge that contained a small table with a sign indicating that a continental breakfast was available at 7:00 a.m. There was a television and a chair on which was seated a strange looking woman in a housecoat staring wild-eyed at the newscast on the screen.

To my right was the service counter. The woman standing behind the counter seemed to be in her late sixties to early seventies. She was thin, but she looked strong. She didn't smile. She merely looked at me with stern, grey eyes and asked, "Can I help you?" For some unknown reason the thought popped into my head, *Holy crap! That's gotta be Mother Bates Jr.! And this must be the Motel Bates Jr.!* I didn't scream. I didn't run. I just looked out the window and saw the snow falling harder and harder and the sky getting darker and darker. I turned to Mother Bates Jr. and said, "I need a room."

Unfortunately for me, my room was on the lower floor which seemed to be one long, dark basement lined with evil looking doors with evil looking numbers. At the end of the hall, I saw a large, shadowy figure slowly shuffling toward me. Now maybe the large, shadowy figure wasn't really coming toward me. Maybe it just wanted to watch TV with the wild-eyed woman in the dimly lit lounge. I didn't care. I got to my room as fast as I could.

I opened the evil looking door to my room and stepped inside. Everything in the room was dark in color so much so that even with every light on, the room was still dark. I closed the door and immediately noticed that not only was the door's security swing bar missing, the chain guard was missing as well! I'm not lying! I immediately propped up a chair under the door knob and wedged a shoe in the door's hinge pin stop in such a way as to force a killer to break down the door instead of using the key like I was positive Mother Bates Jr. was planning to do.

I opened the curtains to look out the win… *dammit!* I thought to myself. *This is a freakin' basement!* There was a window, but it was five feet off the ground, only a foot high, and there was no way to open it. I stepped on a chair to get a clear view (I'm only 5'4") and noticed that the view was of the area behind the motel at ground level. It was dark outside and the snow was blowing furiously. The wind was howling (really!) and all I could see was snow and impenetrable blackness. I was starting to get scared.

I went to the bathroom to wash up and that's when I noticed a sign on the door that read, "Please close bathroom door when taking a shower or the fire alarm will go off." This seemed to translate roughly to "Please close the bathroom door when taking a shower because we need to sneak in without your noticing us which is helped by the fact we removed your door chain and we wish to stab you repeatedly and steal your belongings."

I was dead tired and knew I needed to sleep but I was just too nervous. I pulled out my pocket knife and placed it under my pillow. I climbed into bed fully clothed and didn't get under the covers in case I had to react quickly to the appearance of a serial killer.

Somehow, I dozed off but the howling wind outside and the strange laughter inside (really!) kept waking me up every hour on the hour. Finally, 4:00 a.m., I bolted out of bed with knife in hand and exclaimed, "To hell with this! I'm getting out of here!" I didn't care if I died in the blizzard. I wanted to get as far away from that motel as possible. I grabbed my stuff, dropped the key on the front counter, jumped in the car and sped off into the blizzard and toward a frozen demise. I really didn't care.

The snow was still coming down hard and I couldn't see the road very well. I just followed the tire tracks of the cars that had gone before me. The snow finally cleared up around eight and I started to finally relax. After stopping to eat, I hit the road again. I was little tired, but in good spirits now that fear and danger were far behind me. Then, in the distance, in the west, a little south of the interstate, I saw a black tower.

What in the hell is that? I thought to myself. It was creepy looking and suddenly I was filled with foreboding. The tower was pretty far off, but it stood out, dark and evil looking. And what was it with all of this dark and evil stuff I was encountering on the trip? I concentrated on driving and listened to some CDs. Every time I started to relax, I looked down the road and the black tower stood there. It was getting closer and closer and creepier and creepier and I was getting nervous again.

Eventually, I got close enough to the tower to see a road leading from it to the highway. I decided not to go there. I started to calm down again when I saw a road sign. The sign read, ENTERING THE CRAZY MOUNTAINS.

The Crazy Mountains?!!! Are you kidding me? I thought that it had to be a joke and looked ahead. There, right there, looming in front of me was a mountain range. It was a big and dark and evil looking mountain range. Above the big and dark and evil mountain range was a blizzard. It was starting to get dark. *Lord protect me*, I prayed.

The only way I can describe that harrowing portion of the trip is to put it in terms that people can understand. Imagine that you're driving around and suddenly you find yourself on the wrong side of town. You've never been there before and it's starting to get dark. You want to get out of there but there's only one road back to safety. Now imagine that night has fallen. It's pitch black outside except for your headlights. It's snowing like crazy. The road starts getting icy and it starts climbing up at a ninety-degree angle. Now you're a zillion feet in the air. Now the road starts zigzagging all over the place. Now you can't see the road because of the snow. Suddenly the freezing, twisting, snow covered road starts descending at a ninety-degree angle. You're on the slow lane riding your brakes and praying you won't fall off the edge of the mountain. You see a sign to your right that says, RUNAWAY TRUCK RAMP. You think to yourself, *the ramp is on my side of the road! If there's a runaway truck back there, it's going to come down my lane! Shit! Damn! Hell!* Now repeat this about seventy times over a five-hour period. All during that five-hour ordeal, you have to piss like a race horse.

I don't remember exactly how long it took me to get through the Crazy Mountains. I only remember the road getting less crazy and I had time to observe the cars around me. A lot of them had bumper stickers that I didn't read seeing as I was concentrating on not getting myself killed on the road. I saw a sign for Coeur D'Alene, Idaho was up ahead about fifty miles. I didn't know why, but my spider sense was tingling. I forgot the tingling when I saw the rest stop I had been praying for.

I stopped.

It was pretty hard to get out of the car since my hands were locked in a death grip on the steering wheel. I walked through the snow to the restroom, not paying attention to the people around me. I peed for what felt like ten minutes and planned my next move which would be to sleep about five hours at the rest stop and then make it to Bremerton.

As I walked to the car, I finally noticed the people at the stop. They were all white. Several of the men had shaved heads. All of them were staring at me. They didn't look friendly. I then noticed some of the cars in the parking lot sported White Power bumper stickers. Suddenly I remembered where I heard of Coeur D'Alene. It was a documentary on neo-Nazis and skin heads. I thought to myself, *Holy crap! I'm a brown guy and I'm surrounded by white supremist iceholes!* Needless to say, I decided that it would not be in my best interest to spend the night at a rest stop surrounded by a pile of white power freaks especially since my brown skin against the snow made for an easy target. I hit the road and drove the remaining 360 miles to Bremerton stopping only for gas and a burger.

When I reached my daughter's place, my two grandkids, The Pup and Menkey Boy, were waiting for me. I think I said something like, "Arr nyuk rokrok sploink" and passed out for fourteen hours. The few days I stayed there were refreshing, and I had a blast with the kids. I knew I had a long trip back to San Antonio, so I left with five days before I had to be back at work which would give me some time to wind down. This time I had some company since my youngest son, Eddie, would be with me.

The drive was pleasant except when we went through Los Angeles. Once we got to Arizona, we started having fun. We stopped at The Thing museum which is a hoot. In New Mexico, we came to a rest stop that looked like an adobe hacienda. I made up my mind that should I ever get rich, my house will be designed like that rest stop.

I decided that we would spend the night at The Flying J truck stop in El Paso which is about 560 miles from home. Eddie had a burger and I had a slice of pizza and a beer. Around ten p.m. I started to get sick. I thought it was the pizza and decided I needed some fresh air, so I drove off into the night with the windows rolled down and my son asleep in the back seat.

I stopped at the first rest stop and puked my guts out. I stayed by that toilet for almost an hour. I was sick and wanted to get home. I couldn't sleep. I drove on and stopped at another rest stop and puked. I kept drinking water because I hated the dry heaves. After two hundred miles, I knew it wasn't the pizza that hit me. It had to be appendicitis since I was really hurting.

Eddie told me that maybe he should drive so I could rest, but driving kept my mind off the pain. I was fully aware that appendicitis is not a good thing and I needed to get to a hospital, but I didn't know where to go and I didn't want to be hospitalized in a strange town. I drove on with a few puking breaks while my son stared at me with fear in his eyes. I arrived at Wilford Hall Air Force Hospital around twelve hours after I first got sick.

As I lay waiting for the surgery, I saw a doctor wearing a surgical mask coming toward me. I was in pain but whatever was in the IV had me feeling better. I was getting groggy and I was reflecting on the Big Trip. I looked at the doctor and imagined how this tale would have ended if it was a movie:

Doctor enters operating room.

Our hero looks up and thinks the doctor's features are strangely familiar.

The doctor places his hand on Gil's shoulder.

The doctor speaks, "Well hello, Mr. Polanco! I'm Dr. Bates Jr. and Mother Bates Jr. sends her regards."

The screen goes black.

THE BLOOD PUMP

There comes a time in everyone's lives (if they live long enough) that the thought of mortality comes creeping into their unwilling minds. Now there are those times that one faces life-threatening things like car accidents, stabbings, and angry girlfriends that can make one think, "Holy smacky! I could've died!" While those kinds of things let you know you can croak, they are also things that some people get over because they realize, "Son of a biscuit eater! I'm alive!" The thoughts of mortality that I'm talking about happen when your stupid body starts doing stuff that just ain't right because it never did that before

Now that time that I drove from El Paso to San Antonio with appendicitis was surely the first time I faced mortality because a useless part of my body was trying to make the rest of my body useless. Let me tell you, that was scary. What was scarier was, while I was in the hospital, I learned that I was old and overweight.

Years of enjoying the yummy goodness of refried beans and their evilly delicious companions contributed to my cholesterol reaching a healthy level of 5,278.3 (after fasting). I gained quite a bit of weight, so I decided to try to get back into shape. At 6:45 a.m. on June 12th, I was in the middle of some crunches. I don't know where the crunches came from but there they were and I was in the middle of them.

Being in the middle of crunches can be sweaty and tiring so my breath muscles started circulating a bunch of air. I was making all sorts of sounds. Suddenly, my blood-pump went "SQUEEZE!" Well, let me tell you, I just freaked out all over the place.

My brain-muscle says to me, "I think my blood-pump is crapping out! What would Slackjaw McGoon do in a situation like this?" I then realized that I had no idea who Slackjaw McGoon was, but it was a cool name for a character in a story. I then leaped or leapt (actually I sort of mummy shuffled) to the medicine cabinet and threw, yes threw, five aspirin into my distorted (yet frightfully handsome) face. I then got into my horseless carriage and sped screamingly the one and seven tenths miles to the hospital.

By 7:05 a.m. Doctor Kevorkian Jr. was taking my vitals. I was a bit dismayed about that and asked him if he could leave me with my vitals since I liked them and thought they were vital. He then slinked off muttering, "I never get to have any fun." Seconds later, the real doctor comes to me and says to me, "Son, you're having a heart attack."

The next thing I know, I get stripped down all the way to my glorious naked body and get wheeled into THE ROOM WITH THE THINGS ALL OVER THE PLACE. A lovely nurse lady entered the room, pulled back my cover and proceeded to shave my glorious nakedness. Oh, the humanity!

After the laughter died down, Herr Doktor asked me, "Mein goot friend! Does von pronounce your name 'Gil' or 'Jeel'?" I told that either pronunciation was acceptable since Gil is Amerikaner and Jeel is French because the French can't say "Gil" but they can say "Zheel", but no one can understand what "Zheel" is so the Americanized French rendering is "Jeel", but most normal people just call me Gil.

When the assistants were finally able get Herr Doktor out of the fetal position, I was directed to lie perfectly still. Two kindly looking young medicine guys walked up to me. They had friendly, caring eyes full of concern for my well-being. One of them leaned over and spoke softly in my ear. He said that I had a blockage in my blood pump caused by one too many chalupas at the Taco Cabango. He told me that they needed to stick a catheter in an artery by my groin and gently ram this thing through the catheter all the way through my virgin blood vessels. The thing would then blow up a balloon inside the blockage and shore up the blood vessel with a scaffold called a stent.

The kind medicine guy then told me that I would "feel a bit of pressure" in the area near my groin when they started the procedure. Let me tell you, when a doctor tells you "you're going to feel a bit of pressure" he really means that it's going to hurt to the point that you'll be speaking in tongues and not very nice tongues at that.

After the screams died down, I could see Herr Doktor shoving this wire thing in the spot where I felt the "bit of pressure" and could see on the monitors the thing going into my blood-pump. Herr Doktor told me that I had a 99% blockage and he was going to clear the blockage and put in a stent. I could see the balloon thingee going into the blocked area and then I heard Herr Doktor say, "Inflate."

Yaaaaaah! Don't inflate! Don't inflate! Holy crap! It felt exactly like the heart attack! I think they inflated about three or four times. I lost track of time and must have passed out because the next thing I knew, I was laying in CICU (whatever that means) and I was plugged up to a whole bunch of stuff. I was told that I had to lie perfectly still for the next four to six hours.

A lovely young nurse came into my room and told me I needed to take some pills but that I wouldn't be allowed to sit up to do it. She put four pills in my mouth and attempted to drown me as she poured water into my gagging throat. When the pills finally went down, the lovely (but evil) nurse sweetly informed me that someone was coming in to remove the catheter from the artery by my groin.

She explained that because the catheter was large and I had been given blood thinners, if they just pulled it out I could bleed to death. To prevent me from croaking that way, they were bringing in a young lad who would apply direct pressure to the artery for approximately twenty minutes after pulling out the catheter, so I would have a chance to clot. She pointed to the area where the pressure would be applied. I suddenly remembered a self-defense instructor telling me that spot was known as a "pressure point" which, when struck properly, can bring down the meanest guy on the block.

As I was thinking about the pain I was about to go through, a Neanderthal walked in and said to me, "Me take out catheter in artery by groin now. Geel will feel a bit of pressure." The beast's thumb was jabbed at the exact place my instructor said would cause the most damage. The screams were incredible.

I stayed at the hospital for a couple of days. All during that time, I was bumming out. You see, despite being out of shape, I've always been a pretty active guy. Yeah, much of that activity was around eating and drinking, but my main love is music and playing music. I'm a drummer. Yes, I know the joke that a drummer is a guy who hangs around musicians. We can argue over whether or not drummers are musicians later (meet me in the alley behind the dollar store on Marbach Road next Saturday at 1:00 a.m.). Either way, I was worried that having a heart attack would prevent me from playing drums again.

When I finally saw Herr Doktor, I asked, "Herr Doktor, will this have any effect on my drumming?"

Herr Doktor just smiled at me and said, "Only if you practice. Only if you practice."

3 NONSENSE

I like to write down stuff because I like to remember things that I either make up or actually experience. The Concession is an experience that countless movie goers have experienced. I remember as a kid in the 1960's, a couple of bucks could get you a double feature with popcorn, Milk Duds, and a Dr. Pepper. Today's concession operators should be arrested for price-gouging. To forget crap like that, I often think of stupid stuff like The Metaphysics of Pizza. I forget how it started, but I was in on some online pizza discussion and the spirit of Aristotle took over and I grabbed my copy of Metaphysics and a bottle of whiskey and that was that.

THE CONCESSION

This conversation took about 19 years ago at a movie theater on the Westside of San Antonio. I took my two youngest children to see a movie and the admission price was pretty outrageous. I then went to the concession stand to get the kids some goodies and this is what transpired:

EMPLOYEE: May I help you, Sir?

ME: Sure! I would like your special on three medium popcorn, three candies, and three large Dr. Peppers for $279.95 please!

EMPLOYEE: I'm sorry, Sir, but this theater chain does not carry Dr. Pepper and the special is good only during the matinee. The evening price is $427.32.

ME: What? What?!!! You don't carry Dr. Pepper?

EMPLOYEE: No, Sir.

ME: Okay, then make it three Big Reds.

EMPLOYEE: Sorry, Sir, but we don't carry Big Red.

ME: Excuse me, but what PLANET is this?

EMPLOYEE: Earth.

ME: And what COUNTRY are we in?

EMPLOYEE: Texas

ME: And what do Texas mommies wean their children on?

EMPLOYEE: Dr. Pepper and peanuts?

ME: That's right, Mister! And what do you suppose would be a favorite junk food snack for the beautiful Brown People of the Great State of Texas?

EMPLOYEE: Big Red and Doritos?

ME: Very good! I see you're not a total maroon after all. You're still dumb as a post, but it's not your fault. You're probably from up North, huh?

EMPLOYEE: Yah, yuh betcha.

ME: Look, Buddy, this is TEXAS! Since the time that Cabeza De Vaca discovered the two springs from which The Doctor AND Big Red flow, providing their life-giving, spirit-enhancing, gas-producing essences to all Texan creatures, great and small, we Texans have had the God given right; I repeat, THE GOD GIVEN RIGHT to life, liberty and the consumption of Dr. Pepper and Big Red!

(The applause from the crowd that gathered was deafening)

EMPLOYEE: I feel your pain, Sir, but we still carry only Pepsi products.

ME: All right. Then just give me the damned Pepsi.

EMPLOYEE: That'll be $427.32, Sir.

ME: Here ya go, ya damned communist. You ain't seen the last of me!

EMPLOYEE: Yah, yuh betcha!

I can tell you this much, I've been renting movies a lot more lately. With a 50" screen, no one blocking my view, microwave popcorn, a case of Dr. Pepper, and a pause button, I'm a lot calmer now.

METAPHYSICS OF PIZZA

I was having a lively discussion with some friends regarding the properties of a good pizza. As is the case with most philosophical jousts, the friends I was with were in a slightly enhanced mental state brought on by the consumption of maybe a beer or two. I think the discussion started with one philosopher asking, "If a pizza falls in a forest and no one is around to see it, will the delivery guy still get a tip?"

That question naturally led to other questions about pizza. It got to the point that some in our group began to question the very existence of pizza itself. I felt obliged to make an attempt at swaying the doubters and convince them that the full feeling in their stomachs and the pepperoni and cheese remnants on their tomato sauce stained beards were, in fact, physical evidence of a pizza's passage in temporal space.

I explained to my colleagues that while most mammals would think that the existence of pizza is self-evident, I could neither prove nor disprove the existence of pizza because I am human, mortal and prone to err. And yet I, being that I am what I am and that's all that I am, prefer to believe that pizza exists in both the physical and metaphysical sense. The sheer enjoyment that is attained from the consumption of a tangible or imagined object seemed to demand that I should uphold the honor of the sacred pizza.

The question was asked why I, who am "of the Mexican persuasion" (as one friend put it), should rush to the defense of a real or imaginary food stuff that is not of Hispanic origin? Of course, any person of any education at all would immediately realize that the person asking that ignorant question was a buffoon without the slightest knowledge of the pizza's revered history and, most probably, a racist. I responded (very slowly) that pizza has been thought to have originated in the New World in the form of the tostada.

The Europeans really liked the tostadas and one of them (a conquistador named Mendigo Mendoza) sent the recipe to his Italian cousin Alfredo Fettuccine. Alfredo was a renowned for his poor memory and habitual drinking. He worked part-time as a body double in the illicit and scandalous Teatro di Porno. His stage name was Creamy Alfredo. Some people drink to forget, but Alfredo was already a forgetful drunk and passed on an incomprehensible tostada recipe to Gino the Lip who happened to be the proprietor of the Leaning Tower Café in Pisa.

Then again, we must consider the evidence that pizza is as old as civilization and may have actually originated in Sumer as evidenced by the newest translation of the Sumerian Kings List line 334: "Then the army of Gutium was defeated and the pizza was taken to Unug."

Now you, dear reader, are aware of this well-established fact but you may wonder why I believe that pizza exists. To that I reply that my certitude of pizza's existence is the direct result of intense study and years of research. I can honestly tell you that I base my belief on the work of none other than the Great Philosopher, Aristotle. We know that the Philosopher's work on Metaphysics as published is incomplete. Several of ancient manuscripts refer to yet undiscovered lost lines in Logic under Categories, Metaphysics Book IX in the discussion of potency and actuality, and let's not forget his Short Physical Treatise: On Pizza.

Let us consider Aristotle's wisdom and try to understand the pizza as he saw it. We must understand that while the internet did not exist in Aristotle's time, it doesn't necessarily mean that he was unable to research and network with other sandal wearing brainiacs. It's evident that he knew a lot about pizza. Take for example his observations of pizza development in Egypt:

"Now that practical skills have developed enough to provide adequately for material needs, one of these sciences which are not devoted to utilitarian ends has been able to arise in Egypt, the priestly caste here having the leisure necessary for pizza research."

Aristotle's own extensive study into the very essence of pizza resulted in the following observations:

"The whole pizza is more than the sum of its parts."

"The so-called Pythagoreans, who were the first to take up mathematics, not only advanced this subject, but saturated with it, they fancied that the principles of pizzas were the principles of all things."

"We cannot ... prove pizza truths by arithmetic."

"The chief forms of beauty are order and symmetry and definiteness, which the pizza demonstrates in a special degree."

"There are things which seem incredible to most men who have not studied pizza."

"That which we must learn to do, we learn by eating pizza."

"The pizza is that which is divisible into indivisibles that are infinitely divisible."

"The gods too are fond of pizza."

"Hippocrates is an excellent geometer but a complete fool with a pizza."

How much more proof does one need to acknowledge the existence of pizza? I could go on and on about Aristotle's pizza lectures and how I came to believe wholeheartedly in the existence of pizza. But proving it is another matter since minutes after we see it, all that lies before us is an empty box which leaves us thinking, "Was there really a pizza in that box, or did I imagine it?"

4 IN THE NAVY

I served in the United State Navy for twenty years and pretty much had a blast. Yeah, it wasn't always "Fun Time Navy" due to family separations and several near-death experiences but I have to say that I had plenty of adventures that are hard to forget. Princess Li and her Magic Muffin, The International Incident of Samoa, waking up on the wrong ship, The Taiwanese Unintelligible Lunch, The Caning of the Stripper by the Other Stripper, The Five Thousand Screaming Tasmanians, King Tut's Condom & The Back of His Head, The Secret Service Pen Knife and Bill Clinton are just a few tales I need to write about, but that's for another book.

The following two stories happened in 1981 while I was stationed onboard the USS LONG BEACH (CGN-9) when we were in dry dock at Bremerton Naval Shipyard. The first story deals with unintentional chemical warfare and the second is about a spirit who didn't like a shipmate that I didn't like.

THE GREATEST FART

Farts are wonderful things. Yeah, they tend to stink. In fact, they're sometimes downright horrendous. The thing about farts is that everyone does them. Kids fart. Boys fart. Girls fart (even though they don't admit it). Moms fart. And Dads are the All Time Kings of Farts. I have a lot of experiences with farts. Heck, the fart battles I had with my brother Eddie are the stuff of legend.

Now I could go on and on about farts and I know that everyone has a great fart story. I have a million of them. Eddie, who is five years older than me, used to bear hug me, fart, and then pull me into the insidious fumes that flew from his butt. Since I wasn't big enough to do that to him, I got revenge by getting a paper bag. I stood in front of him, put my butt in the bag, farted a big fart, closed the bag, and walked straight up to him.

He looked at me and just busted out laughing. He was laughing so hard he couldn't move. I held the bag in front of his face and popped it. The fart contained in the bag was pretty stinky. It was really bad. When the gas was released, Eddie started gagging but he kept laughing and choking at the same time. In retrospect, I think I could've killed him if I had eaten more chili with chocolate milk. I'm glad I didn't kill him because he's a pretty good big brother.

This story has nothing to do with my brother and our fart wars. Even though there were some incredible battles, I'm not sure they produced the greatest fart. There are some farts that everyone remembers. I know I've thrown at least two or three that are still talked about in different parts of the globe. There was one fart of mine that I believe is true Hall of Fame material.

I was stationed aboard the USS LONG BEACH in the winter of 1981. The ship was in dry dock in Bremerton, WA for overhaul. Most people don't understand what a sailor's life is like. It isn't easy. We generally work an eight to twelve-hour day and, depending on the ship, we have to stand twenty-four-hour duty every three to five days. We were in four section duty in Bremerton.

Every day, Reveille is held at 0600 and we have to get up for chow. At 0700, the crew musters for quarters with their respective divisions. Inspection is held, and the Plan of the Day is read to the division. On the weekends, only those personnel going on duty and the guys going off duty have to muster. Off duty personnel get to sleep in.

I was in Admin and our department head was Warrant Officer Lassiter. He wasn't too bad as officers go, but he was pretty hardcore about maintaining discipline in ranks during muster. Let me tell you, if anyone so much as blinked during muster, he'd rip them a new ice hole faster than you can scream, "Mommy!"

I wasn't new to Washington State. I did a year and half overhaul with the USS MARVIN SHIELDS in West Seattle a couple of years earlier. I loved Seattle. There were a few Korean bars I used to hang out at like The Tokyo East which boasted a sign that read, "Two Pool Tables – Girls To Play With", The Arirang featuring Mister Lee and His Magic Organ singing really bad covers of really bad American songs, and Nikko's Oriental Garden (my favorite hangout).

Nikko's was real cool because it was a go-go bar. No, the girls weren't topless. It sported two dance stages where bikini-clad Korean and Vietnamese girls would gyrate to songs played on the jukebox. There was a dance floor, two bars, and a room in back that sported two pool tables. The back stage had a large window that allowed the pool players to look at the go-go girls. I had known a few girls at each of the bars and made friends with the managers and owners. There was one girl in particular that I became very close to as a friend. Her stage name was Mona.

When I first saw Mona, I was stationed on the USS MARVIN

49

SHIELDS (FF-1066) when we were in dry-dock in Seattle. She was a dancer. My buddy John and I were scared of her. She was a good-looking woman, but she wasn't dainty like the other girls. She had a great body, but it was the kind of body that was big and strong. She looked like she could take Conan the Barbarian home and leave him crying for his mommy. Yeah, we were scared of her, but we were fascinated just the same.

One night, John suggested that one of us should buy her a drink. I told him, "Go for it," and he paid the bartender for a glass of wine while Mona was at the back stage. We were playing pool watching Mona dance and John went to go take a leak. The drink arrived while John walked back to the pool room. Mona got off the stage, hugged me and said, "Oh! Thank you for the drink!" John was a little perturbed and said, "Hey! I bought the drink," but Mona kept smiling at me all night.

I never dated Mona, but we became close friends. She always would warn me about the different Korean girls I dated. She would say stuff like, "Geel, you need a nice Korean girl. These girls no good for you!" She wanted me to meet her cousin who never did come to the US. When I came back to Washington two years later, Mona was an assistant manager at Nikko's.

I should say that hanging with Koreans is an olfactory ordeal because they love to eat kimchi. Kimchi is a Korean delicacy. It's a cabbage dish that's fermented and smells like rotten death that had been festering in the butt of a three hundred-pound Mongolian wino for a month. It's delicious.

One particularly cold Saturday, I decided to go to Seattle. I had duty the next day, but I wasn't scheduled for watch and, since it would be Sunday, I knew all I had to do was make muster and then I could sleep all day. With this knowledge and fifty bucks in my pocket I intended to get trashed.

Man, it was *cold* outside. Seattle, being Seattle, was wet. It was windy. It was real windy. It was real windy and real wet and real cold. For those who've never spent a winter in Seattle, I must warn you to wear about seven layers of clothes and strap spikes to your shoes. Even though it doesn't snow a lot and the temperature on its own isn't particularly breathtaking, the wind roaring through the Puget Sound comes straight from Alaska at about 7,000 miles per hour blowing the little frozen drops of rain in a horizontal assault that feels like you're in the middle of a hurricane on Pluto. Black ice forms everywhere and it can be pretty dangerous to drive. Walking the streets can be an adventure. The sidewalks become ice skating rinks. The experienced pedestrian just stands straight, opens his trench coat and lets the wind blow him to his destination.

As I walked into Nikko's, noticed that Mona wasn't behind the bar. She was sitting at a table and stood up to greet me. She was wearing a black skirt and red top. She was made up real pretty. Conan the Barbarian was one lucky man. She gave me a big hug that cracked only two of my ribs and said, "Geel, I been waiting for you!"

It turned out that it was one of the very few Saturdays she was off, and she wanted to have fun. She smiled and told me that she wanted to have some fun and Nikko's wasn't the place to do it. We took off and got into her car. We skidded the four blocks to The Arirang.

It must have been party night because the place was packed with Koreans. The entertainment for the night was, as usual, Mister Lee and His Magic Organ but this time he had a full band complete with backup singers. I have to say that I've always been treated well at The Arirang because I had helped the manager out one night when her previous bar caught fire. She kept my pool cue behind the bar and my first beer was always free.

Coming in with Mona was a different story. I didn't know it at the time, but she was respected and maybe a little bit feared. She was, after all, a black belt in Taekwondo and apparently part of the local hierarchy. The table by the stage was immediately cleared of an unlucky couple. We were seated and, without Mona saying a word, a big bowl of kimchi, two bowls of rice, a jar of hot sake, and two small cups were placed on the table. We were treated like royalty.

Mona can be a hard woman. I guess she had to be in her line of business which is why I was surprised when she picked up my cup and the jar of sake in a slow and artful way as she smiled at me with genuine kindness. She said in a gentle voice, "Geel, you are a special man" as she slowly poured the sake into my cup and handed it to me. She filled her cup, lifted it up in a toast and said, "Topshida." She then became a girl ready to have some real fun.

I sipped the hot sake because I wasn't used to it. Mona downed it in one gulp. She picked up her chopsticks, grabbed a big pile of kimchi, placed it on top of my rice, and then served herself. "Let's eat," she said and then proceeded to shovel the kimchi and rice into her mouth in a most unladylike fashion. Actually, there's no way to eat kimchi and rice in a ladylike or gentlemanly way. You just hold the bowl up to your face and scoop the mixture into your mouth. You keep shoveling until the bowl is empty and then take a shot of sake before you take your first breath.

"I *love* kimchi!" Mona exclaimed. I love it too and this kimchi was topnotch. It was crisp, hot, and particularly stinky. We polished it off as Mister Lee took the stage. We also finished the jar of sake. One of the girls immediately brought us another jar and a bowl of little dried fish. The band started to play a disco song and we got up to dance. We danced all night. Whenever a slow song was played, she took off her high heels, so she wouldn't tower over me. If I didn't like Mona so much, I would've fallen in love with her that night.

We talked and laughed all night while the staff kept bringing us more sake and kimchi. I know we had at least four servings of kimchi and the sake… well I lost count of the jars we drank. By night's end, I was on my lips, but Mona seemed unaffected. She poured me into her car and drove me back to Bremerton. I don't' know how she did it. She gave me a little kiss on my cheek and said, "Geel, I had a good time." I did too. If I was a foot taller and built like a tank I would've married her but only a Mongol king built like the Hulk with the drinking ability of W.C. Fields and the heart of Lancelot could ever deserve a woman like Mona.

0600 came too early for a guy who spent an entire night eating kimchi and drinking sake.

The Navy tends to pack enlisted personnel in really cramped berthing areas. Our racks (bunks) were stacked three high and I had a middle rack. The racks all had privacy curtains and we slept with the curtains closed. I could hear my shipmates getting up, but I was far too messed up to move. I figured I would, skip breakfast, wait till 0745 to get up, put on my dungarees and go to muster.

Unfortunately, I felt a horrendous rumbling in my intestines. It was bad. What was also bad was that I felt like my blood had been replaced by turpentine. Every nerve in my body seemed to have been injected with a combination of Clorox and mud.

My eyes were burning coals and the sand that sealed my eyes shut had hardened like concrete. I slowly took my left hand and peeled open one eye. There was a really bad taste in my mouth. Someone decided to make a paste of bile, rotten fish, and hippopotamus poop, spread it on my tongue and seal my mouth shut. I opened my mouth to breathe and the stench that emanated from my piteous maw turned my stomach. I shut my mouth really quick to stop the smell before I puked in my rack.

My intestines were churning. Inside I knew I held a cesspool of unspeakable horror and a festering bloating carcass that was about to explode. I had to fart. I had to fart badly, and I knew that if I farted in my rack with the curtains closed I'd probably die from the noxious fumes. I was too hung over to get up and so I reached behind me with my left hand, pulled open the curtain, stuck my butt outside and let out a *psssst!*

Unbeknownst to me, one of my buddies who slept in the rack beneath me had just gotten up and was putting on his dungarees. His unfortunate face happened to be caught smack in front of the open curtain and my gaseous behind. All I heard was, "Oh, God!" and then there was some wretched gagging. I heard him run to the head to puke. "Sorry, Dude," I croaked.

I felt like hell. I knew I had to get up to make muster or I'd be in big trouble. I slid out of my rack, pulled my t-shirt on inside out, put on my dungarees, sort of tucked in my shirt, put on both my working jacket and pea coat since it would be freezing outside, pulled my wool watch cap over my uncombed hair and hobbled outside to muster. Somewhere in the back of my mind I knew that Mr. Lassiter would hold inspection and write me up for looking like hell. I didn't care.

The off-going and on-coming duty sections assembled topside in three ranks. It was freezing cold. Lucky for us, there was no wind, but we were shivering just the same. I stood in the center of the middle rank because I didn't want Mr. Lassiter to start chewing me out the second he saw me. One of my friends, Doug, looked at me and said, "Gil, you look like crap!"

I started to say, "I know," but, as soon as my mouth opened the stench made him turn green. "Oh, man!" Doug moved to the third rank to get away from me.

Warrant Offer Lassiter arrived, and the section leader called us to attention. He held muster, and everyone was present. He usually would hold inspection and then the section leader would read the Plan of the Day before dismissing us but since it was so darned cold he told us he'd forgo inspection and get on with the Plan of the Day. Lucky me.

We had to stand at attention while the POD was being read by the section leader with Mr. Lassiter staring at us to catch any unfortunate sailor who blinked or had to sneeze. We were statues. We were freezing statues.

We were freezing and shivering statues.

It was so cold, it felt like I was standing outside in my skivvies. I was numb. I wanted to get back to my rack ASAP, but the section leader just took his sweet time reading, "Blah, blah, blah." I knew I would die from hyperthermia. Then the kimchi and sake came to my rescue.

The rumbling in my intestines was getting really bad and I knew I needed to fart. I also knew that if I let out a big kaboom, Lassiter would have my butt. Unfortunately, the green gaseous horror was expanding to the point that I could not contain it any longer.

Now I know for a fact that every living being on the planet farts. Humans happen to be the only ones who try their best to keep it secret when standing in a crowd. We all have our methods and usually it involves squeezing our butt cheeks tightly and slowly letting out the gas so as not to make a sound. This results in what is infamously known as the SBD.

I was freezing, and my guts were burning.

"Blah, blah, blah…"

Mr. Lassiter stared at us daring anyone to move.

"Blah, blah, blah…"

I pinched my butt cheeks and slowly released the gas. *Psssst!*

"Blah, blah, blah…"

My pants suddenly felt warm. No, I didn't crap myself, but the gas was warm, hot even, and I felt the heat slowly making its way up my pea coat. The gas came in a continuous *psssst* and flowed through both of my sleeves warming my arms. *Psssst!*

I felt the heat come out the bottom of my pea coat warming my legs and out of my collar warming my face. I knew it smelled bad, but I didn't mind because I was warm. I kid you not, the *psssst* lasted for at least a minute.

"Blah, blah, blah…"

Psssst…

I heard a cough behind me.

"Blah, blah, blah…"

Psssst…

I heard a cough in front of me.

"Blah, blah, blah…"

Psssst…

Everyone in formation began to fidget and cough. Mr. Lassiter raised a quizzical eyebrow obviously wondering what the heck was going on.

"Blah, blah, blah…"

Psssst…

It was too much for the guy standing next to me. "Sploink this squoyt!" he yelled and ran from ground zero as fast as he could. That was the signal for the entire duty section to scatter in all directions for safety. I'm talking *everyone*, even the section leaders. There was hacking and gagging and cussing and stuff.

Mr. Lassiter had a shocked look on his face. You know, one of those *what the* looks. He took one step toward the vanishing formation. He raised his hand with an index finger extended and said, "What the…" and stopped dead in his tracks.

His face turned pale as he landed smack in the middle of my internal death blossom.

"…. flud!"

Mr. Lassiter ran faster than I've ever seen him run.

Let me tell you, I've had my share of experiences during my naval career. I've had ups and downs. I've had my share of awards and even had the honor of laying a wreath while in Pearl Harbor with President Clinton. I don't think anything really compares to the glory of that freezing day in Bremerton.

That day, against all odds, during a deadly gas attack, while all hands ran from certain death to save their pathetic lives, I, Petty Officer Polanco from San Antonio, Texas, did not break ranks. I stood tall. I stood proud. And feeling warm all over, I smiled.

THE SMOKING GHOST

There are so many stories I can tell. Many of them are unbelievable because of their fantastic and sometimes strange nature. They can seem unbelievable because they always seem to happen to me. I'm in the mood to tell one of those stories, so here I sit in my garage with a notepad, two fingers of Weller on the rocks, and a Punch Rothschild billowing clouds of great Dominican tobacco smoke.

It's hotter'n Heck in San Antonio. Hundred plus and the summer has just started. I could go inside but it just feels better out here. The box fan keeps the dry air circulating while Levon Helm sings "When I Go Away" on the CD player. I look out front and see some kids taking turns on a mini bike. My dog, Fugly, is lying under my pickup. He looks at me as if to ask, "When in the *Heck* are you going a plant a shade tree out here?"

That damned ice cream truck is once again coming down the street blaring an obnoxious and inane jingle through thirty-year old loudspeakers giving the godforsaken tune a piercing quality that can only be fixed by a well-placed sledgehammer. That SOB doesn't have the courtesy to turn the thing off when someone is buying an ice cream or raspa. It's hard to think. If only he'd play something good like a little Traveling Wilbury's.

So now I'm thinking of "The End of the Line" video with the rocking chair rocking itself to the disembodied voice of Roy Orbison. And this reminds me of my ghost story. I served in the Navy for twenty years and during that time I've seen some mighty strange stuff. One of the strangest times was when I was stationed aboard the USS LONG BEACH (CGN-9) from 1980 to 1983.

I find it funny that a lot of sailors hate sea duty. I personally enjoyed being at sea. I had served earlier on board the USS MARVIN SHIELDS (FF-1066) which was a Knox Class Destroyer. We didn't destroy much of anything while I was aboard except for a Taiwanese tug boat in Keelung, Pier Two in San Diego, and the Surfside Club in Western Samoa, but that's a whole other story. Anyone who knows me knows that I'm a tin-can sailor at heart.

The love I had for the seagoing life led me to reenlist for guaranteed duty to the LONG BEACH (CGN-9). She was the last of the true cruisers although there are some who would argue that the distinction belongs to the TRUXTON. She was a nuclear powered, guided missile cruiser with the fire power to level a small planet. She was impressive.

She was so impressive, my Dad had an 8X10 of the LONG BEACH hanging on the wall with his own Navy photos even though he never served aboard her. I jumped at the chance to serve on the ship whose motto was "Strike Hard, Strike Home." I couldn't wait to get underway with this great ship. It had been about two years since I'd been at sea and I couldn't wait to deploy. Man, I was excited.

I spent about two months TEMDU at NAVSTA San Diego on 32nd Street waiting for my orders. I really liked that base, especially the bowling alley which was the home of The Big Bowler, one of the best burgers I've ever eaten in my life. One day, Chief Napasindayao called me to his desk. "Hey, Petty Officer Polanco! Looks like you really lucked out." *Yeah, I get to deploy soon. WESTPAC, here I come!* "The LONG BEACH is pulling into Bremerton for overhaul. She'll be in dry dock for two years."

"Aw, what the flud...!"

There wasn't much I could do except report to the ship that we would call "Building 9" and hopefully get at least a shakedown cruise out of it. Turns out, I really enjoyed my tour. When I arrived at the Bremerton Naval Shipyard, the LONG BEACH was already in dry dock. I stared at her in awe. At 721 feet and 15,540 tons, she was five times as massive as the MARVIN SHIELDS. The Petty Officer of the Watch informed me that the crew had already moved off the ship and that I was to report to Building 32. I checked in at the Personnel Office which was to be my work center. Quinn, one of the PN's, checked me in and led me to a barge.

What the Heck is this?

"This is home for the next two years," Quinn said. I surveyed the barge and was real disappointed. I went through a yearlong overhaul with the MARVIN SHIELDS and the crew was put up in some pretty nice double-wide trailers that were almost livable. This setup was like being onboard a poorly maintained WW I ship that was welded to the pier. I figured I could put up with it since I didn't make a lot of money and I spent most of my off time in Seattle any way. I didn't decide to move off-base until one fine Saturday afternoon.

As was the case any time I had duty on a Friday, I changed into my civvies right after Saturday morning muster and headed straight to Seattle where I'd have breakfast and coffee and walk around the Pike Place Market. Most of my shipmates who lived on the barge would hit the rack and wouldn't leave until it was time to party at the clubs. It was starting to rain pretty hard that morning, but I didn't care.

I had planned to spend the morning and early afternoon wandering about and just doing stuff. I wanted to get back to the barge about four, eat dinner, shower, shave, and head back to Seattle for a night of debauchery. As I got back to the shipyard, I noticed a pile of sailors and yard workers on the pier. I also noticed that the barge was not where it was supposed to be. It was out in the harbor being towed by a tug boat.

To make a long story short, I found out that the heavy rains that morning came with heavy winds. The weather got to be so severe that the barge broke away from the pier about nine in the morning. About half of the crew was cast adrift. Since it was a Saturday and no ships were scheduled to come in, there were no tugs manned to do anything. All the tug crews were civilian, so it took quite a while to man a tug to rescue the barge. Needless to say, by the time the barge was tied to the pier again (6:00 p.m.) there was a pile of ticked off sailors scrambling to get ashore. I decided right then and there that I was going to move out in town.

I had two buddies, Al and Dan, who decided to move off the barge with me. We rented a small house (a really small house) out in town. It worked out okay for a while but, the constant parties played hell on the poor guy who had duty on a weekend and had to wake up at six in order to make muster by seven. Two months of this convinced me to move out and find a place of my own.

I lucked out and found a studio apartment complex on Burwell just across the street from the side gate of the shipyard. The complex kind of reminded me of a one story motel set up. As I recall, there were three rows of eight apartments with a "courtyard" in between each row. I had the second apartment in the middle row. I had a restroom with a shower, a small kitchen, and a good-sized living room with a sleeper sofa. My back door opened to one courtyard and the front door to the other courtyard. I paid $75.00 per month. I loved that place.

I had a shelf for my books and albums and a table for my stereo. I bought a hibachi to grill my hamburgers on Saturdays. The place was full of characters right out of a trailer park movie. Tanky Talbert lived in the apartment right across from my back door. He was a shipmate of mine who was an amateur boxer. He had a gold tooth with a "T" engraved in it. He was a darned good welter weight and was recruited by the Navy boxing team, giving him a chance to go to the Olympic trials but he hated the Navy and got out to make it on his own. He was my Best Man at my wedding. He liked expensive things. He bought a Cadillac but couldn't afford the gas to drive it. He bought alligator shoes and really nice clothes but couldn't afford to go out. I asked him, "Tanky, why in the Hell do you spend all of this money when you can't go out and show it off?"

"Dis muthafludda may be broke, but dis muthafludda looks good," he told me. I really miss him.

My other buddy, Dan, moved into the first apartment across from me. We drank a lot outside my front door. One day, we were drunk and listening to Frank Zappa when this girl with purple hair wearing a skin tight, pink, leopard print leotard, with high heels asks us for a cigarette and a beer. She proceeded to spill the beer on Dan's lap and when he asks why the hell she did that, she responds, "Because I want to lick it off." She then licked the beer off Dan's lap. Her name was April

One night, I got back from Seattle and as I walked past Dan's place I heard a violent commotion.

Slap! Bang! Slap! Slap!

"Call me a biscuit!"

"You're a dirty, sploinking biscuit!"

Slap! Crash! Bang! Slap!

"Yes! Yes! Yes!"

"Lap it up like a starving kitten!"

"Mew! Mew!"

Holy squoyt, Dan! I didn't know you had it in you!

I went inside and got some sleep. Then about four in the morning, I hear a knock on my door. *What the flud?* I peeled open my eyes and opened the door. There, standing there with torn clothes, messed up hair, drenched with sweat, reeking of sex, and mascara running down her face, was April. "Can I sleep here with you?" she pleaded.

"No."

I slammed the door in her face and went back to sleep.

One day, as I was getting off duty, I get a base-wide message that anyone coming in contact with a young, purple-haired girl should report to medical. It turned out that it was April and she spent a week in the officers' quarters and several of them came down with the clap. I ran home and then went to Dan's pad. I showed him the message.

"Holy mackerel!" he screamed. "My manifold of love is going to fall off!"

Dan's manifold of love didn't fall off. Turns out he didn't get the clap at all. Boy, was he lucky.

Okay, now I'm starting to reminisce. There is so much to talk about that place and I'm veering off-subject. When I first moved in, I was ecstatic. This was my place. I could do pretty much what I wanted. The fridge was full of beer and other nutritious stuff. I kept it clean and was really surprised to see cigar smoke about six inches thick covering my entire ceiling when I got home after work. I was more surprised to see the smoke disappear in a matter of seconds.

I didn't smoke cigars back then, but I liked the smell. I wondered who it could be in the complex that smoked cigars? I forgot the incident in a couple of days.   Then one night, I went to bed early because I was real tired. I slept like a rock. I was lying on my back when something woke me up. I opened my eyes and saw cigar smoke on the ceiling. I sat up and the smoke was gone but the cigar aroma remained. Things like this happened every other day.

I thought that maybe there was a crack on the wall and my neighbor's smoke was coming through. I went to the manager and told him about it. He said that there was no crack in the wall. The studio next door was unoccupied, and the geeky sailor next door didn't smoke.

I know that "geek" is an overused term but there is no other way to describe this guy. He was pretty scrawny. It looked like he had cartilage instead of bones. He was pasty white with sandy blonde hair and he wore thick glasses. He didn't go out. He didn't have a girlfriend, but he informed me one day that everything for him would change.

He showed me a letter. It was an acceptance letter from his *mail order bride!* I was flabbergasted. He showed me her picture. She was real pretty and she was arriving in a week! I must say that she was prettier in real life. She was Filipina with long, straight, black hair, beautiful skin and big, beautiful, brown eyes. I didn't see much of them since they never went outside.

Yeah, he wasn't the kind of guy to smoke. I asked the manager how the heck could cigar smoke get into my pad? He was hesitant to answer. He then told me that the guy who rented the studio before me died in his sleep. He was a heavy cigar smoker.

Wow. That was freaky. Well, I wasn't scared if all the ghost did was smoke cigars. After a while, I just got used to it. I got used to a lot of things. Things like April who constantly wandered around the complex wearing tacky, revealing clothing. I got used to the smoking ghost and tried to learn more about him. The only thing I learned was the ghost got pretty spooky if he didn't like someone. That someone was a shipmate of mine that I didn't particularly like. To protect his privacy and pride I will call him "Bob."

Bob had to buy friends because he was an icehole. He was somewhat of a racist and I found it strange that he would periodically want to hang with me. One day he walked into my pad since both the front and back doors were open. Even though I didn't like him, I don't believe in acting like an icehole. "Want a beer?" I asked.

"Sure!" He sat down and laid a camera and flash on my kitchen table.

"You know a lot about camera equipment?"

"Yeah, a bit"

Handing me the flash, he said, "This flash doesn't work."

I replaced the batteries, tried it out and nothing. I hooked it to my camera. Nothing. I took out the batteries and laid the flash on the table. "Looks like you have to get a new flash, Bob," I said.

"Squoyt! That's fluddin' tee up!"

All of a sudden, the flash went off.

We both jumped. We were both freaked out because there were no batteries in the flash and it wasn't connected to the camera. Bob wondered how in the heck could something like that happen. I thought that maybe it was the ghost having a little fun with us. I told him the story about the cigar smoke. He looked at me in disbelief.

"That's a bunch of boosh-squash! There's no such thing as ghosts!" He went on to disparage me and my beliefs. Then he pointed his finger at me and said, "You're full of quiche!" Right then, the flash went off like a strobe light. Flash, flash, flash!

"Muthaflu…"

Bob was gone in a flash.

"Thanks buddy," I said to the ghost. "I don't like him either."

As you can see, the ghost didn't scare me at all. He didn't bother me. He was kind of part of the furniture. He also didn't do anything when other people were around either; except, that is, when Bob came around. Now one thing that did scare me was Lee. I have to tell you about Lee.

I love music. I most especially love jazz. Not that Kenny G type of crap. My collection at that time included Miles Davis (of course), Herbie Mann, Brian Auger, Maynard Ferguson, Weather Report, Return to Forever, Herbie Hancock, John Coltrane, The Jeff Loerber Fusion, Al DiMeola, The Mahavishnu Orchestra, Stan Getz, Flora Purim, Thelonius Monk, Shadowfax, Acoustic Alchemy, Al Jarreau, Raashan Roland Kirk, Keith Jarrett, and a pile of others. I liked to put my speakers outside, sit out front with a beer, and play music all day long. The neighbors were cool with it and often would join me for drinks and music.

I think I had been in the apartment about a month when I first saw Lee. It was a Saturday afternoon. I was kind of broke and had just enough money for a case of Old Milwaukee, a loaf of bread, two packs of Marlboros, and half a pound of hamburger meat. Dan had duty and most of the tenants had gone to Seattle or Tacoma, so I had the courtyard pretty much to myself.

I was cooking a burger on my hibachi, listening to tunes, and drinking a beer when I noticed the new tenant in the fourth apartment across the courtyard from where I lived. He was big. He was Black. He was bald. He looked strong and he looked mean. He was doing a soft-shoe dance by his front door. I realized that he was dancing to the music I was playing.

He danced for about three straight hours, going inside only to get a drink. At one point, he stopped dancing and walked straight to where I was sitting. He stopped and stood right in front of me.

He was bigger and blacker and balder and stronger and scarier than any man I'd seen in my life. I felt my balls go into my throat. He looked just plain mean and he wasn't smiling. He spoke in a deep voice like Barry White only not as romantic.

"Who the *flud* are you playing?" he asked in a tone that sounded like he would snap my neck if I gave the wrong answer.

"Uh, Brian Auger's Oblivion Express – Live Oblivion," I squeaked.

He shook his head up and down and said, "That's some pretty good squeesh." He walked back to his place and kept dancing.

About six o'clock, I decided to go inside and watch some TV. I cleaned up my mess outside and turned off the music. I closed the door. Right at that moment, there was a banging on the door. I looked outside, and there he was all big and black and scary.

"Did I tell you to turn that quiche off?" he growled.

"Uh, no, Sir," I whimpered.

"Well, put that quiche back on. What's your name, boy?"

"G-G-Gil, Sir," I responded.

"Don't call me sir, muthafludda! My name is Lee!"

I put the music back on and he went back to dancing all night long. Eventually, everyone in the complex wound up in the courtyard and partied like maniacs.

I found out that Lee was on parole. He had been in prison for murder, which made him even scarier. For some reason, he liked me. I'd play music and he would dance outside of his apartment. Sometimes he'd bring me an album to play. On my birthday, he brought me a bottle of whiskey and told me that if anyone ever messed with me he would kill them good. I thought as long as I kept him dancing, nothing could go wrong.

One day, my geek neighbor with the mail order bride knocked on my door. Turned out he had temporary duty orders to a school and he'd be gone for a week. He told me that I was the only one in the complex he could trust and asked me to keep an eye on his girl to make sure nothing bad happened. Heck, it wouldn't be a problem, so I told him not to worry. Turns out I was the one who needed to worry.

The bride always stayed inside, and I would check to see if she needed anything. She never went outside. I think I was the only one who knew she was there. I was wrong. A couple of days before the geek was to come back, I decided to go to the store and pick up a few things for the payday party that we always threw at the complex. As I walked up to my place, I saw something that sent chills down my spine, up my scalp, down my legs, and around my oompah loompahs.

Standing by her door was the mail order bride. She was holding a small package of groceries. She was trembling. She was looking up. What she was looking at was Lee and he was leaning against her door blocking her way. He was leaning down and talking to her in a low voice.

Holy quiche! Oh flud! What the hell is going on?

I steeled myself and walked up to them not sure of what was going to happen. I could see the poor girl was scared out of her mind. Her eyes were wide with fear. Lee had a lecherous look on his face. He was smiling. He was saying, "Baby doll, you are way too fine to be fluddin' around with that skinny little white piece of quiche. He ain't no man. You need a real man."

Aw squoyt! He's going to rape her! I have to do something! I'm going to fluddin' die!

"Uh, Lee…"

Without looking at me, Lee grabbed my arm with his giant iron hand and pulled me between him and the girl. "This is a real man, Baby Doll. His name is Gil. He's got style. Not like that white crinkle you're with. He's a Mexican and I hear they sploink good. Don't you, Gil?"

"Uh."

"Shut up. I'm helping you out here. Take her inside and start sploinking."

"What?"

"You heard me. Take her inside and start sploinking. If I don't hear you sploinking, I'll come in and sploink you both myself."

I opened the door and Lee gently pushed us both inside. "Now you two have fun."

I closed the door behind us and could see behind the curtain that he was standing guard outside. The poor girl was clutching her bag to her breast and shaking like a leaf. I knew I had to do something or something bad was going to happen.

I went to the sleeper sofa and pulled out the bed. I looked at her and she was crying as she started to undo her blouse. I put my hand on hers and shook my head. "Don't," I said. "Sit down on the bed."

I sat next to her and started bouncing up and down on the bed. She looked at me with a puzzled look. "Go ahead," I said, "he'll think we're doing something." She started to bounce. We could see his shadow through the curtain and he was shaking his head with approval. She started to laugh. I laughed, and we bounced on the bed for all we were worth. After a while, we heard him exclaim "Now that's what I'm talking about!" He left.

We kept bouncing for a few more minutes just to be safe. I lead her to my back door and looked to see if anyone was watching. The coast was clear. I walked her to her backdoor. She smiled at me and, with tears in her eyes, she kissed me on the cheek. "Thank you," she whispered and went inside.

I stepped back inside my pad and noticed cigar smoke. I figured the ghost was probably having a good laugh at my expense. Now I never had any conversations with the ghost and he never tried to contact me. Sometimes I would get a feeling of being really relaxed when I saw the smoke. I'm not sure how to explain this but, when I walked back inside, the studio seemed a little brighter. The place just felt happy. I felt happy. It felt almost as though I was getting a pat on the back for a job well done. Maybe what I felt was the joy of not getting killed by Lee. I like to think that the ghost approved of what I did.

Of course, the ghost probably didn't approve of everything he saw. I was only aware of one thing that the ghost didn't like. That thing was Bob. I hadn't seen Bob since the camera flash incident and I had put it completely out of my mind.

One Saturday morning, I decided I was going to record a couple of albums on cassette. I had one of those record player/cassette recorder combo stereos that allowed me to record directly to cassette. The stereo had no external microphone, so I didn't have to be quiet during the recording process.

For those of you who are unfamiliar with cassettes or albums, the recording process is a little tedious. Unlike digital recording where one only needs to copy and paste a file, recording an album to tape requires you to play the entire album, ensure each song is free of dust, stop the record player & cassette at the end of the first side of the album, turn the album over (and cassette depending on length), clean the album so there are no crackles, and record the second side. After the recording is complete, you then have to listen to the entire tape to make sure everything came out right. Once that's done, you want to prevent accidentally recording over the music by punching out two little tabs on the spine of the tape.

The albums I recorded that day were "The Romantic Warrior" by Return to Forever and "Second Wind" by Brian Auger's Oblivion Express. In case you haven't noticed, I'm a Brian Auger freak. I had just finished recording both albums and punched out the tabs before I listened to the tapes. It was about 1:00 p.m. and I put on the Brian Auger tape. I grabbed a beer and sat down to listen. Just about that time, Bob walked into my place (since I had both front and back doors open). Since I try not to be an ice-hole even with people who are ice-holes, I offered him a beer. I didn't bother to turn the player off.

I forget what we were discussing when Side A of the tape finished. I flipped the tape and started playing Side B. I remember Bob said something that ticked me off. It was a bad joke about Spics. Now I'm not overly sensitive about my ethnicity like some people I know. I mean there are some pretty funny ethnic jokes out there that anyone can laugh at but there are some that are just plain offensive. He was in the middle of the joke, when, all of a sudden, we heard some voices.

The voices got louder and louder. It almost sounded like someone was arguing next door but that wasn't the case. We noticed that the voices were coming out of the stereo speakers and the music was starting to fade as the voices got louder. We soon realized that the voices were ours and the conversation was from the time Bob had walked in a half hour earlier.

"Hey! How'd you do that?"

I was flabbergasted. "I didn't do that," I said.

"Boosh-squash! You were probably recording us when I first came in."

I explained to him that it was impossible for me to accomplish such a thing for the following reasons:

1. The stereo had no external mic.
2. The stereo had no internal mic.
3. I had previously punched the tabs on the tape to prevent recording over the music.
4. The stereo wasn't a multi-track recorder so there was no way to fade a music track while recording vocals simultaneously.
5. The recording was of the conversation from when Bob first came in. Since I was playing Side A at the time, the recording should've been on that side. Instead, it was on Side B.
6. The recorder can only record on the playing side, but even if it could record on the other side, the recording should have been backwards and towards the end of the tape on the B side.

Needless to say, even I was creeped out. The only logical explanation was the ghost was screwing with us. Well, Bob would have none of that business and called me a liar and a carp hole. He kept going on and on and I was starting to get pissed off. About that time, we both noticed the smell of a cigar. There, on the ceiling was a thick layer of cigar smoke.

"Son of a biscuit eater!"

Bob bolted out of my place. He never spoke to me again. That was a good thing.

About twelve years ago, I went back to Bremerton to visit my daughter who was living there at the time. I drove by the old apartment complex, but it had been torn down. It really bummed me out. I went to one of the new local taverns and had a beer. I thought about Tanky, Dan, April, Lee, and some of the other characters I grew to know and love. I lit up a cigar and remembered the ghost. I never knew his name.

5 MUSICAL STUFF

Music has always played a huge part of my life. My mom's side of the family is to blame. My grandfather and my uncle Gil both played guitar. Another uncle played accordion. Anyone who knows me knows my brother Eddie is a flippin' guitar meister. I've been playing drums for a bit and have had quite a few musical experiences myself. The first piece is my response to the question, "Why do drummers play with their eyes closed?" The second story is about being my brother's brother and witnessing an epic battle. The third tale is about my childhood friend, John Gilbert Ruiz and the embarrassment he unwittingly caused every guy in school with his trumpet playing.

THE PLIGHT OF ALL DRUMMERS

As a short, Catholic, retired Navy, Dallas Cowboy loving, meat eating, Kenny G hating, anti-socialist, old Brown Guy I can honestly say that I'm pretty used to abuse. Now I'm not the type that constantly whines about real or imagined abuses (the whining you hear from behind my bedroom door has more to do with the withholding of sexual gratification than actual abuse, but now that I think of it… it really is abuse). I do have to say that I belong to a group of human beings from all walks of life that have commonality in that they, above all living beings, have been the recipients of the vilest forms of abuse. Yes, folks, I'm talking about drummers.

Drummers have been abused ever since Grog Krupa of the Squatting Rabbit Clan played his first drum solo before a crowd of vegetable and rock throwing Neanderthals. Drummers always have the most equipment to haul. They must arrive at a show at least an hour before the other band members otherwise they'll be given a ten-inch square space on a forty-five-degree incline on which to set up their thirty-seven-piece kit. That space will (without fail) be the one space that either has no shade, has a hole above where the rain is pouring down, or has a nest of angry wasps directly over the drums. And the jokes! There are more drummer jokes than there are lousy guitarists. The number of abuses suffered by drummers is vast but they all pale in comparison to that most vile abuse of them all: Man Ass.

I'm serious about this! I've been playing drums for a few years and my band mates keep their backs to me every single night. There may be some hot chicks out in the audience, but do I ever get to see them? Noooooooooooo! I have cymbals to the left and cymbals to the right. They do a good job of blocking the view. To the left of the cymbals will be a bassist so that view is blocked. To the right of the cymbals will be the guitar player so that view is blocked. The only unobstructed view I ever get is dead center and that is blocked by the lead singer who insists on being smack dab in the middle. After the first hour, the band starts getting sweaty. Some bands get sweatier than others. Heck! The only things I ever get to see are my cymbals and the sweaty, gyrating asses of the band. It's enough to drive a drummer bonkers! It's no wonder so many drummers want to learn guitar.

Pretend for a moment that you're a drummer. Close your eyes and imagine that most horrific of our travails: constant visions of the nightmarish repugnancy of sweaty, quivering, steaming man-ass blocking the view of the far more lovely girl-ass gyrating with sensual glee in front of the stage as the owner of the aforementioned steaming man-ass poses so as to prevent the scantily clad groupie from viewing the devilishly handsome drummer who now closes his eyes to protect his mind from disintegrating due to the shock of the forced viewing of man-ass, clenching his teeth from the agony of being deprived of girl-ass viewing and from the offal filled stench of the steaming man-ass before him which now moves aside so the lovely scantily clad groupie can now view the drummer whose normally radiantly handsome, chiseled features are now twisted from the mental, physical, visual, and nasal torture of viewing man-ass whereupon seeing the drummer's abnormally contorted features, the lovely groupie gasps in revulsion, turns again to the singing man-ass while the poor innocent drummer plays on, unaware that respite from the pitiless man-ass was but a glance away.

That's why we play with our eyes closed.

GUITAR BATTLE

Music has always been a part of my life. I'm just goofy for it. My first conscious memory of music was of a guy playing flamenco guitar when we were living in Barcelona. I thought it was pretty neat. I really liked watching the beautiful women dancing and spinning so their dresses went up and I could see their legs. I may have been only five years old, but I could certainly appreciate a nice set of legs.

When we moved back to San Antonio, music started to play a dominant role in my life. My parents used to drag me downtown to see Vicente Fernandez or Pedro Infante or any number of Mexican singers who happened to be in town. If we weren't at some music show, we'd be at some kind of dance featuring a conjunto playing polkas, rancheras, or cumbias. Sometimes, we'd go to my uncle Gil's house and he'd play guitar. Uncle Frank played accordion. My grandfather played guitar. In fact, it seemed that over half of my Mom's side of the family played an instrument. Mom's voice was beautiful.

With the plethora of Mexican music surrounding us, it's funny that my Dad was a huge fan of Country and Western music. Every time we were in the car, he had the radio tuned to KBER which played a lot of Country music back then. My brother, on the other hand, listened to KONO and KTSA which played the pop music of the time. Back then, "Pop" covered everything from bubble gum to jazz to rock.

I still remember Ed's first guitar. I was in elementary school. It came with a book and an instructional record. Mom and Dad wanted him to play it but he said he needed to clean it or something. Later that night, I woke up and heard Ed's record player. "This is how you tune a guitar…"

Over the years, Ed became a San Antonio guitar god. His bands included The Saints & The Sinners, Suburban Expressway, Amethyst, Sandra's Tea, Island, and Eddie & The Allniters. I've lost track of how many people he's played with and in how many venues he performed. He's simply a great guitarist. I don't say that because he's my brother. I say that because it's true.

When I was in school, people were always coming up to me and saying stuff like "you're Eddie's little brother" or "your brother kicks ass." Sometimes people wouldn't talk to me, but they'd point at me and tell a friend "that's Eddie's little brother." Every once in a while, I'd get a "so do you play guitar too?"

No. I don't play guitar. Well, maybe just a little. I play drums. With the exception of a couple of short stints with Rene & The Royalties and Man's Freedom when I was a freshman in high school, I didn't start playing until my mid-thirties while in the Navy. When I retired in '96 The Whitinos, the band I was in, did a stint in San Antonio. Shawn "Sly McGee" Clark (guitar) and Brian Annett (bass) left after a few months and returned to Minneapolis. Since then, we've gotten back together enough times to record a CD we call "Heathens Rejoice!"

After my friends left, I was without a band, so I started hanging out at blues jams to sit in whenever I could. "Hey! You're Eddie's little brother!" Damn. Here we go again. It seemed like every blues or rock guy in town knew Eddie, and I was his little brother. I needed to find my own niche where I would be known as "Gil" and not someone's little brother.

I started playing with a band called Blue Bonnet Plague, but they broke up a few months after I joined the band. My friend David Rodriguez asked me if I wanted to start a new band and I thought why not? We formed True Stories which opened up an entire new world for me.

Playing all over town in dives and some pretty nice places, True Stories connected with a whole pile of musicians. I was fortunate enough to have some of those musicians contact me to fill in for AWOL drummers from time to time. Eventually, I started getting my name known as a pocket drummer who played with several bands. It was kind of neat to earn my own reputation without people knowing that I was Eddie's brother. The thing is, in San Antonio, musicians cross paths and genres and inevitably I crossed musical paths with Eddie.

Now don't get me wrong. I'd been on stage with Ed before during open jams or if his drummer couldn't make a show. I think one of the coolest experiences I had was the time Ed was booked to open for Omar and The Howlers. He wanted to do a three piece with acoustic guitar, keyboard, and snare. He wanted me to play. Man, it was great. He also asked me to work with him on a Robert Johnson tribute CD called "Hot Tamales – A San Antonio Tribute to Robert Johnson" on Bexar Nekkid Records. Let me tell you, that was freaking just as great.

Now Ed and I, living in different musical worlds, have a mutual friend in Ray Symczyk who just so happens to play guitar, accordion, piano, mandolin, trumpet, drums, bazuki, and I think he may even have a Vulcan harp hidden in his closet. Ray and Ed had played together for a long time and people who've seen them trade guitar licks often stare in slack-jawed amazement.

Ray plays with countless bands and True Stories was lucky enough to be one of those bands. One of the songs we played was "Like a Hurricane" by Neil Young. Ray would shred on lead. We'd let him loose until he signaled us with the hook and then we would end the song. It was always a hit with the audience.

One day, Eddie asked me to bring True Stories to the Overlook where he was playing, and we could do three or four songs. The place was packed, and we did three songs which were well received. The third song we played was Dylan's "I Shall Be Released" which we do with a bit of a reggae feel. Eddie really liked it and joined us on stage. We were getting ready to leave the stage when Eddie said, "Hey! Do one more!"

Dave, John, Ray, and I all looked at each other and we knew that having Eddie and Ray together on stage was not to be wasted. Dave smiled and called out "Like a Hurricane". We were rocking the hell out of that song. When we got to the last part of the song where the lead guitar takes over, all hell broke loose. Eddie and Ray were trading solos with the intensity of a great tennis match where the fans can only move their heads back and forth to observe greatness in action. Those two guys were so amazing that the rest of us in the band could only stare. I think that lead trade off added about six minutes to the song.

Dave, John, and I were having a blast but were starting to wonder when Ray was ever going to cue us to end the tune. When it finally ended, and the applause died down, Ray looked at Dave and said, "I forgot I was supposed to end the song!"

I think that convinced Eddie to do a stint with us (he later played on our Estilo San Antonio CD) which was really neat. The highlight of that stint was a show at an icon of live music, Taco Land. It was one of those places where the beer was cold and cheap, and the bands never made much money, but it didn't matter since it definitely was the coolest venue in town.

True Stories shared the night with Los #3 Dinners (a party waiting to happen) and the place was packed. We were pretty much rocking the place and having a great time. It was time for us to do our last song which was, of course, "Like a Hurricane" and, to tell you the truth, no one expected the fireworks that erupted on that stage. It was like a world championship wrestling match between Screaming Ray Symczyk and Edible Ed Polanco.

I can't adequately replicate the entire song in words, but I'll try to get the tail end of the guitar battle with an approximation of the guitar sounds and their translation:

RAY - deehr deedeedeehr deedeehr deedeehr deehr deedeehr deedeehr… deeh deedeedeehr deedeehr deedeehr deeeeeeehrrrrrrrrr… (translation: Alas, Edible Ed! You have met your match!)

ED –Wrrrrrang! tringtringtingiling whank whank woka woka brrrrrreeeeennzzzzzz! (translation: Oh yeah? Don't give me no mess!)

RAY - * trilla trilla yeeeeeeeeeeeeeeeeeee blinblinblindinity kwoki drizzzzzzz (translation: Insipid oaf! Ye hast besplattered me! Take this!)

ED – (Rolling up his sleeves) * Kwwweeeeeeek! Kah wahwahwah blmoiunsaiwoajfa#$ blit yaaaaaa eeeeiiiiyaaaaa drrrrreeeeng spoit (Translation: And STAY down!)

Ray, looking bloody and stunned, somehow climbed the top turnbuckle and delivered the Twirling Telecaster Atomic Drop Kick. Ed, looking like a Picasso meat sculpture, countered with the Ibanez Death Grip. Oh, the humanity! The stage looked like a battle field with picks laying cracked and broken, mewling pitifully for a guitarist to pick them up. Reverb fluid was splattered everywhere and was ankle deep in some places.

The screams were incredible.

After we tore down and put away our instruments, I went to the bar to get a beer. Eddie and Ray were sitting and talking while waiting for Los #3 Dinners to come on. I overheard some people talking about our last song.

"Hurricane really kicked ass!"

"Yeah! That guitar battle was something else."

"I know Ray, but who's the other guitar player?"

"That's Eddie. He's Gil's brother."

Yes, he is.

COLOUR MY WORLD

There are times when a friend does a particularly notable thing that makes you and your other friends look like complete weenies. That friend was John Gilbert who I met in the second grade. We were best friends and he had the embarrassing habit of hugging me every time he saw me on the playground. He was like that; always hugging people, especially me. I would push him away and say, "Hey, man! Cut that out!" He would then laugh and say something like, "What's wrong with hugging a frieng?"

No, that's not a misspelling. "Frieng" was just his goofy way of saying, "friend."

John Gilbert wasn't gay. Heck, we didn't know what gay was back then. We knew that there were guys on television that our parents called "flamboyant" and Bernie, who owned the flower shop on the corner of Cupples and Bedford, was certainly "flamboyant." The older kids used to call them "jotos." There was one kid in the neighborhood that we thought might be a joto because he was always wearing short shorts and flip-flops. John Gilbert wasn't like that at all. He just liked to hug people.

There was one person he *really* liked to hug. That person was a girl and that girl was Sylvia. Now, he didn't start liking to hug her until we were in the eighth grade. When we were in elementary school, she wasn't particularly pretty, and she was a bit mean. She was probably mean because I made fun of her and once I hit her with a rock. She was fast and strong and grabbed me by the arm, spun me around like a rag doll a couple of times and flung me what felt like fifty feet. I think that throw could've won her the gold in the hammer throw. Instead, it won us a trip to the principal's office where I had to apologize for being a moron.

Sylvia really changed in junior high. She went from being a creepy girl to becoming a Girl. All of the guys started to notice her but, before he started to notice her, John Gilbert noticed another girl we called "Trog." Trog was short for troglodyte which was a pre-human creature that Trog resembled. Even John Gilbert called her that, so we had no idea why he liked her.

One day, John Gilbert noticed Sylvia at the cheerleader tryouts for Brentwood Junior High. He was smitten. He soon lost interest in Trog and so we got our friend, Mugs, to set them up. It was a relationship that was to last well into high school.

Before I go into their relationship and the notable thing John Gilbert did that made all of the guys in school look like weenies to all of the girls, I should mention that he was a study in contrasts. He was short; about five feet three. He was built like a fire hydrant and stronger than many guys twice his size. He knew karate and broke things like boards and bricks and stuff. He was pretty tough and wasn't scared of anything. Scratch that. He was scared of essays.

On the flipside, he was in the school band and could play a mean trumpet. He really was pretty darned good. His heroes were Doc Severson, Bill Chase, and Maynard Ferguson. Of course, like any horn player of the day, he learned to play all the tunes by Blood, Sweat, & Tears and Chicago. He also had a voice like you wouldn't believe. Boy, he could sing!

I remember one time when I was in the Navy, I came home on leave and stopped by to see John Gilbert. He was in a band called "Canela" and he wanted me to check them out at a club on the West Side. The place was packed with young couples dancing the night away. John played trumpet and did backing vocals. He sang lead on one song.

Angel Baby was a favorite of lovers everywhere. The dance floor was jam-packed once that song started. It was Slow Dance Heaven. Like many dance bands in the 70's, Canela extended the song with a solo (in this case, a soprano sax) and all of the couples held each other tight with their eyes closed. After the solo ended, John Gilbert launched into the final verse in a range that would've left Frankie Valli crying in a corner. My jaw dropped. I looked around the dance floor and every couple had stopped dancing and looked at the stage. His singing was electrifying. No one moved until the end of the song and the entire club erupted in a sustained ovation. During the break, I told the guys how amazing the song was, and I'd never seen anything like it. One of John's band mates told me, "Man, that happens every time he sings that song."

Back in junior high, John decided to join the choir. I forget the choir teacher's name, but she liked John and convinced him to try out for the talent show. When he told me about it, I was a bit concerned because he played trumpet and a trumpet player alone on stage in front of a bunch of junior high kids is not a very smart trumpet player. I mean, I know that I would never make fun of him, but the rest of the kids could be merciless. I asked him what he was going to play, and he said, "Colour My World" by Chicago.

Sweet biscuits! What in the hell was he thinking? Yes, Chicago was a horn band, but that song was for piano, vocal, and flute! What's more, "Colour My World" was one of the sappiest love songs ever recorded. The girls *loved* that song. It certainly wasn't a guy song. What's worse, he was going to do the flute solo on trumpet *and* have the choir teacher accompany him on piano? I begged him not to do it. He would be the laughing stock of Brentwood Junior High! He didn't listen to me.

The day of the talent show arrived and we all gathered in the cafeteria to jeer the hapless "talent" on display. It was a pretty dismal show. The chorus of boos and laughter went on non-stop. John Gilbert was on last. I said a silent prayer for him.

As he stepped on stage, holding his trumpet, I could hear the giggles in the crowd. When the choir teacher came up and sat behind the piano the laughter really started. John wasn't fazed at all. He stepped up to the microphone and said, "I want to dedicate this song…" *no, John, no!* "to my girlfriend, Sylvia, the most beautiful girl in the world."

The gasps from the guys were audible, while every girl in the cafeteria sighed, "Awwwwww!"

The choir teacher began to play the piano.

Ding-ding ding ding-ding-ding
Ding-ding ding ding-ding-ding
Ding-ding ding ding-ding-ding
Ding-ding ding ding-ding-ding
Ding-ding ding ding-ding-ding
Ding-ding ding ding-ding-ding
Ding-ding ding ding-ding-ding
Ding-ding ding ding-ding-ding
Ding-ding ding ding-ding-ding
Ding-ding ding ding-ding-ding
Ding-ding ding ding-ding-ding
Ding-ding ding ding-ding-ding
Ding-ding ding ding-ding-ding
Ding-ding ding ding-ding-ding
Ding ding ding…

And then John began to sing.

"As time goes o-o-o-n,

I ree-a-lize
Just what you meeean
To-oo meeee
And nowwww
Now that you're near
Promise your love
That I've waited to share
And dream of our moment togeeetherrrr
Colour my wo-orld
With hopes of loving you…....."

John placed the trumpet to his lips and played like I had never heard him play before.

Daaaa dadadada
Dada da da
Dada da da
Dada da dada da daaa
Dada dadaaaaa
Daaaaaaa
Dada dada da daaaa
Dadadadadada
Daaaa
Daaaa
Dadadadadaaaaaaa

Every guy in the cafeteria sat there with his mouth hanging open. Every girl squealed with delight with tears running down their cheeks. Mascara was dripping everywhere, making every young lady look as if they had taken makeup tips from Alice Cooper. All I can say is, the screams were incredible.

What was also incredible was that all our girlfriends punched every one of us simultaneously and hissed something like, "why can't you do something like that for me!" or "why can't you be that romantic?" or "why can't you be more like John Gilbert?"

Even though he made us all look like a bunch of wienies, we had to hand it to him. John Gilbert had guts. We always respected him but, after that day he was king of the roost for quite a while.

Sylvia broke up with John in high school and it pained him to no end. He was resilient though and was soon hooking up with other girls by virtue of his musicianship as well as his personality. He was a true romantic, but I don't think he ever loved anyone as hard as he loved Sylvia. It took almost twenty years until he found Lilly who taught him how to love again.

As I mentioned before, John Gilbert was a heck of a musician. He was also something of an entrepreneur who knew how to manage a band. He worked his butt off to succeed in the music world. Somewhere along the line, he turned to management and running sound because it made him more money. Eventually, he stopped playing all together.

I joined the Navy before he stopped and saw him only every other year when I came home on leave. We kind of drifted apart for quite a while until I retired in 1996. I was sad to see that he had stopped playing. I remember one time when he pulled out his trumpet and showed it to me. "I can't play anymore," he said, "my lips have gone soft."

I think it was around 1998 when he moved to Oklahoma with Lilly and their little girl. He would come back into town once in a while and we'd party pretty hard. He had been there about a year and stopped by to pick up a little bar that I had refinished for him. We wound up buying a couple of cases of beer. We sat around listening to a bunch of tunes from our younger days and some new stuff we picked up over the years.

I put on a new CD I just bought. It was The Brand New Heavies. He was really taken with it, so I gave it to him. He told me he was starting to pick up the trumpet again and wanted to start a new band. I was so happy. I told him that he never should've stopped because he was one hell of a musician. He told me all about his plans and I told him I couldn't wait to see the new band. When he left, we hugged each other and said our goodbyes.

About a month later, about 2:30 in the morning, I was awakened by a phone call. *What the hell? Who in the heck is calling me at this time in the morning?* It was Lilly.

"Hello?"

"Gil, John Gilbert is dead."

"What?"

"John Gilbert is dead. He had a heart attack."

For a second I thought she was joking. It wasn't a joke. They had just gotten home from a family night out and he collapsed on the floor. I can't describe how I felt. I was in shock. He was only 43 and had so much going for him.

I think about John Gilbert a lot. I'm glad that we were best friends. I'm glad that we were able to talk and laugh together all night long when he stopped by. But my heart breaks because I so dearly wanted to see my friend play just one more time.

6 HEY, ESSAYS!

So, you're at the point in this book where, apart from the occasional letter to the editor, I first tried to present myself as a writer. The Annual Multi-Cultural Conferences held at San Antonio College always had some intriguing themes that often dealt with timely issues. Of course, social issues are fraught with political fights that I liken to a demolition derby between a blind driver and a driver with no arms. Getting on that track was scary but I thought maybe I could bring a different perspective on the derby. The first three essays were my first entries to the conference.

When I published the first edition of For Reals, I had become something of a minor celebrity. I think I had about a dozen fans (not including Mom) that went right out and bought a book. Dr. Daniel Rodriguez bought the book and he asked if I could give a little talk at a National Hispanic Month event held at Palo Alto College. Something to Think About was my way of telling students to discover who they are through research and reflection, not by believing what they're told.

The Suit is a speech I gave for the Thi Beta Kappa induction ceremony for Palo Alto. I was really surprised and honored to be the featured speaker. These kids are like some of the top students in the college because they have maintained a 3.50 grade point average. They're real go-getters and it was really strange that I would be asked to give an inspirational speech. Why strange? I've always been a horrible student and I don't even have a degree.

The Reformed Revolutionary was my last entry for the Annual Multi-Cultural Conference. I wrote You People for the next conference, but I wasn't invited back.

WHAT WALL? GETTING PAST FEAR AND LOATHING

My parents taught me two rules for life. The first was respect and that it should extend to God, country, family, every person I meet and especially me. The second was that I could accomplish anything because only I had the power to prevent myself from success. I have learned many other things during the past fifty years and one is that not all assumptions are correct. That lesson came when I was seven years old.

San Antonio was very different in 1964. Back then the ethnic segregation was quite stark with the Mexicans in the west and south sides, the Blacks in the east and the Whites or "Anglos" as we called them in the North side running the city. Everyone had their place and that's the way it was.

My home was in a neighborhood by Kelly AFB and I attended Brentwood Elementary School. The principal was Mrs. Hoelscher who was an elderly Anglo lady with a kindly face and a right arm that could rattle every bone in an unlucky kid's body with one whack of her one inch thick "board of education." One visit to her office was enough. No one ever went back twice. We heard rumors of a fourth grader who went in a second time and was never seen again.

We were model students.

The student body was all Mexican with a few exceptions. These exceptions were Anglos. We didn't dislike them, but we knew they were different. They always had nice new clothes from Sears or Montgomery Ward and our stuff came from Solo-Serve. We were always dirty from playing "cream the guy with the ball" while they always looked like they just got out of the shower. The one Anglo kid that tried to be like us was Timmy Smith. His name really wasn't Timmy Smith, but I'll call him that for privacy's sake.

Timmy and I became buddies and one day he invited me over to his house to play. My parents gave me permission and the usual orders. I was to always address his parents as Sir or Ma'am, obey the rules of the house, and eat everything on my plate. Arriving at Timmy's house and clutching my one-armed G.I. Joe, I rang the doorbell.

The door opened and before me stood a beautiful lady. She was even prettier than Mrs. Cleaver on TV. She wore a nice dress and an apron. She wore black high-heels and had shiny legs. Heck, even at that age I could appreciate a nice set of legs. She smiled at me, turned around and called out sweetly, "Timmy! Your little Mexican friend is here!"

"Gee, what a nice lady," I thought to myself. She let me in and Timmy called me into the living room.

Some people may think I should have been offended by this introduction, but they seem to forget that things were a bit different back then. As an eight-year-old, I wasn't taught to be offended by imagined slights even though I didn't think I was that little. I was instead dumbstruck by the house I had entered.

The living room had shag carpeting and wall paneling. They even had a *color TV*! There were plastic runners everywhere. The furniture was also covered in plastic. Timmy came in and asked if I wanted to watch TV.

That's when my world view started to disintegrate.

It really didn't bother me that we couldn't sit on the nice furniture since sitting on plastic would be uncomfortable. It did strike me as a wee bit weird to have nice furniture and not enjoy it. I didn't mind having to sit on a little stool to watch TV. What made me realize that all was not well with the Anglos was that the television was tuned to MISTER ROGERS! No kid in his right mind watched Mister Rogers.

Back then there was no cable. We had NBC, CBS, ABC, Public TV, and the Mexican Station. The only time we could watch cartoons was after school from 4 to 5 on weekdays with Captain Gus or Saturday mornings from 8 to 11 a.m. and that was it. Poor Timmy! How could any loving parent force their child to watch Mr. Rogers? Can you say "torture?" Timmy then asked if I wanted to go play in his room. That was fine with me because I hated Mister Rogers, the danged communist. I didn't know what a communist was, but I was sure that Mister Rogers had to be one.

When we entered Timmy's room, I almost fell to my knees weeping in ecstasy because before my eyes stood the fantasy of every boy my age. Timmy had a wall of toys! I counted not one, but five G.I. Joes each one with complete Army Navy, and Air Force uniforms. My one-armed G.I. Joe suddenly seemed like a piece of junk.

I was ready to go outside and play with these wonderful toys but that was not to be. Timmy told me that his Mom didn't let him take any toys outside because they'd get broken. Instead, he had a table set up where we'd play with the G.I. Joes. First, it's Mister Rogers and now this. Father Bill never said Hell could be this bad.

I was so glad when we were called to supper. The table was set like something out of a TV commercial. I knew this had to be good. Once again, I was wrong.

Timmy' family said grace by bowing their heads and praying, "Lord for these gifts we are truly grateful." I thought it was a strange way to say grace and they didn't even cross themselves. I crossed myself as I was taught and noticed them smiling at me. Then I looked at my plate.

There, right before my disbelieving eyes, lay a meatloaf that looked nothing like cafeteria meatloaf. It was juicy and had stuff in it. I didn't know what it was, but it looked weird. The mashed potatoes were lumpy, and it was only later I learned that they didn't always come out of a box.

There was corn mixed with little red things which Timmy's Mom called, "*Mexican* corn in honor of our little guest."

The sickening green things next to the corn turned out to be lima beans. I swear, to this day, I have never again eaten lima beans. I really think there's something seriously wrong with people who like lima beans. They're the kind of people who like rye bread and that was also on my plate. At least I had a glass of Coke to help wash it all down.

I mustered up enough nerve to try the lima beans and immediately regretted it. Figuring that if I mixed all of the food together and ate quickly, the horrible flavors might reach my stomach before my taste buds knew what hit them. I was wrong of course.

Filling my mouth with as much food as possible did nothing to hasten the end of the torture that my taste buds felt. As I polished off the final horrendous morsel, I reached for the salvation of the ice-cold Coke to wash out the taste. As the soda hit my tongue I realized that some things are worse than lima beans. The glass did not hold Coke. It didn't contain root beer either. No, the liquid I was drinking was something called Tab.

I must have blacked out. The next thing I remember was walking home. For the first time in my young life, I no longer envied the Anglos. Instead I felt pity for them and the sad lives they led. They had the nicest things but couldn't use them and their food was terrible.

I didn't have the best clothes, but I could get dirty playing outside and not get in trouble sometimes. I didn't have the best toys, but I could play with them how I wanted. I could watch cartoons and sit on a sofa that wasn't covered in plastic. The beans I ate were good beans and I never had to drink Tab. I was filled with gratitude for being Brown.

I learned from visiting my friend's house that the "grass isn't always greener on the other side of the fence." I also gained a greater appreciation for things I normally took for granted. More importantly, I learned that assumptions made without facts are often wrong.

As minority groups, we get angered when others make assumptions about us that are incorrect. In fact, we can get indignant when that happens. But *we* never make wrong assumptions, do *we?*

We assume that language and culture is racial, therefore any support for a single national language is considered racist. If that is a true assumption, then why is Spanish the national language of Mexico? Was not Spanish forced upon the natives of Mexico? Since most of us with Mexican ancestry trace our blood to the Aztecas, should we not be speaking Nahuatl? There are some who make the argument that Nahuatl comes from Utah and should not be considered the ancestral language of Mexicans but instead be Zapotec, Mayan, Mixtec, Otomi, or Purepecha.

If languages are racial in essence, I must assume that all African-Americans speak Ashanti, Bantu, Dagomba, Dinka, Fulani, Kunama, Malinke, Mende, Suk, Swahili, Wolof and Zulu.

What *is* the language of the White Man? Let's see there's English, Cornish, Irish, Scottish, Welsh, German, Dutch, Finnish, Norwegian, Romanian, Greek, French, Italian, Portuguese and, yes folks, Spanish.

It appears that language and culture are not based on a people's race but rather the region in which that people live. The reason why so many young Hispanics don't speak Spanish is not because of some racist plot but simply the fact that they were born, raised and taught here. They're Americans.

We often assume that Whites are racists and minorities are not. Yet, I don't think I know of any Chicanos who haven't used words like gringo, gabacho, bolillo, negrito or mayate at least several times in their lives. We even use mojado or wetback to describe someone who has crossed the border. The assumption that unlike The Man, we don't use hate speech is also incorrect. Do we not use words such as vendido, coconut, Uncle Tom, Nazi, Fascist, homophobe, war monger, bigot or racist if a person even slightly disagrees with our views?

We assume that we all believe the same things. How many religions do we follow? How many of us even believe in God? How many of us are democrats or republicans? How many of us are for a third party? How many of us believe in rights for undocumented immigrants and how many of us wish we'd concentrate on helping the Chicanos who are already here with illiteracy rates, crime, and teen pregnancy problems? We even have problems deciding what to call ourselves. Hispanic, Latino, Chicano, Negro, Colored, Afro-American, Person of Color, Oriental, Asian... the list goes on.

We seem to be so ready to be offended that whenever we don't like what someone else says we immediately suspect racism is behind the comment. I remember one time I was listening to some music and one of my buddies asked why I never listened to rap. I replied that rap sucks. My friend, who happened to be black, got angry and asked, "What do you have against black music?" My response to the assumption that my musical taste was racist was to show him my collection of music which included works by Miles Davis, John Lee Hooker, John Coltrane, Muddy Waters, Billy Holiday, Herbie Hancock, Stanley Clarke, Jimi Hendrix and B.B. King all of whom are black. I told my friend, "You see, I don't have anything against black music. I only have something against music that sucks."

There seems to be a lack of critical thinking within our community regarding solutions to our problems and the mistaken assumption The Man is keeping us down and setting up barriers that keep us from success. We see a wall and forget that every wall has a door.

Sometimes the door is open. Sometimes it's locked. There are keys to those doors. Those keys are education, training, dedication, desire, communication skills and understanding what is needed to open that door to success. Contrary to popular belief, the doors are not always held open for Whites. If that was the case, all Whites would be successful.

But what do I know?

I'm just another poor schmuck who's trying to earn a living. I know I haven't reached my full potential and that's nobody's fault but my own. I do know that I've had a great life so far. I know that racism and hatred still exist all over the world but they're being beaten every day by people willing to fight mistaken assumptions. I know that I live in a pretty darned good country where I and my children can achieve most anything if we have the will to learn and work.

Yes, there's enough fear and loathing going around that we could feed off them for eternity. If we are to defeat them, we must first defeat them within ourselves. We can start by casting off the assumption that someone is holding us back.

There's a wall over there. I think I see a door. I think I'll ring the doorbell. I might get lima beans and Tab but then again, I just might learn something new.

WHAT COMPLEX?

I'm really getting tired of hearing about the "short man's complex." People make it seem as if every one of us who is not fortunate enough to be a six-foot two Nordic god has anger issues. Perhaps that perception is a direct result of the disdain that the world in general harbors toward men who are physically unable to look down upon other men. The term allows people to not feel guilty over the abuse heaped upon the short.

One may think that I wish for the world to feel guilty for its shabby treatment of the short. Nothing could be further from the truth. I harbor no ill will toward those don't care for short guys. Except for maybe Randy Newman who recorded the song that goes, "Short people got no reason. Short people got no reason. Short people got no reason to liiiiiiiiive!" Now that guy I could do some harm to.

Discrimination against short people and short guys in particular has been a major problem since the Dawn of Man. Even a cursory knowledge of Darwin will prove this point. Is it not relevant that he coined the phrase "survival of the fittest" rather than "survival of the smartest?" Minutes of painstaking research enabled me to discover the origins of the anti-short mentality and the very roots of civilization.

Our early ancestors' most pressing problem was that of survival. Man, being ill equipped to deal with larger, faster predators had to form social groups for protection. It was about 50,000 years ago that one clan solved the problem of survival by accident and gave birth to Civilization.

As we go back in time, we see The Squatting Rabbit Clan arriving at the mastodon hunting grounds. They are late as usual and starving. The ground has been covered in snow for a week and the big animals are on the move to look for a good place to graze. The clan is hungry, and the men need to plan the hunt fast.

Seated around the sacred fire are seven men: Crag Wolf Fang, Urk Bear Claw, Shard Strong Arm, Aton One Eye, Jorg Swift Foot, Dirk Square Chin and Stumpy. Above the men, swinging in a hemp basket is the clan's shaman, Wordorf The Strange. He speaks, "Clan hungry! No eat! Clan die! Clan send five to hunt mastodon. Clan leave one to pleasure women and one to collect wood for cooking of meat."

The first six men merely grunt in response and pick lice off each other's beards. Stumpy is the only one who is deep in thought and forms a plan to kill the mastodon with weapons he has been designing. He knows the plan will work. He stands up and shouts valiantly, "Stumpy lead men on hunt! Bring back much meat!"

Wordorf begins to make strange, unfamiliar noises from his throat that to the group must be a channeling of the spirits. Future generations would identify the sound as laughter, but the clan has never known laughter or humor until now, so it is taken as an omen.

The shaman raises his hand and says, "Hee hee! Uh, ah, Stumpy him short of leg. Stumpy no see above snow drift." The rest of the men commence making the sacred throat sound of their shaman.

Wordorf continues. "Stumpy short of arm. No can throw spear like man. Stumpy throw like little girl." The sacred throat sound from the circle gets louder. "Stumpy no can run. Stumpy go squish under mastodon!" Soon the sacred throat sounds increase as the rest of the clan begins to join the circle.

Stumpy, still standing, responds, "Wordorf wise! Stumpy understand bigger men better to kill big beast. Stumpy stay behind to pleasure women."

Suddenly, the entire clan is seized by spiritual convulsions. They roll on the ground, howling and uttering the sacred throat sounds. They weep, chests heaving, and their sides wracked in pain. Wordorf cries aloud, "Great Spirit! Stop! Make him stop! No can take more! Me sorry Stumpy. Dirk Square Chin stay behind to pleasure women." Somewhere in the dark, twenty female voices whisper, "Yes!"

Stumpy shouts out, "But Stumpy make good axe. Dirk him make nothing! Stumpy smart! Dirk dumb as rock! Stumpy make smart children. Dirk make idiots! Why? Why?"

At that moment, Uma of the Swaying Hips steps forward. She smiles sweetly and says, "Is simple. Stumpy him smart but him short. Dirk him no need brain, him tall, dark, and handsome."

Uma's sentiment has echoed through the centuries to this very day and sheds light on the problems that plague modern man. At the heart of the issue is the fact that we are all animals and, far too often, our instincts get the better of our brains. We gravitate toward that which pleases us rather than that which is good for us. We survived as a species only through the resolve of Stumpy.

A newly discovered cave painting details the disaster of the Squatting

Rabbit Clan's "Mastodon Fiasco" when Shard Strong Arm cast his spear at the lead mastodon. It was at that moment the hunters realized the human arm is not strong enough to throw a spear with sufficient power to penetrate the hide of a mastodon.

The spear bounced off the rump of the beast which turned to charge the hunters. Aton One-Eye, who suffered from diminished depth perception, misjudged the distance from the mastodon. He became known afterwards as Aton The Flat. The hunters returned empty handed except for the remnants of an unfortunate saber-toothed squirrel which was caught in the stampede.

The cave painting shows Dirk Square Chin fathering many large and stupid children while Stumpy was left alone to design the tools that would mean the salvation of the clan. The atlatl was the first of Stumpy's inventions. With this spear thrower, Stumpy single-handedly brought down a bison which immediately made him a hero.

Stumpy's status as hero of the clan naturally made him more attractive to Uma of the Swaying Hips as well as the other women of the clan. Because he was smitten with love for Uma, he offered her the bison's steaming liver. They were immediately married which required Stumpy to invent the barbecue pit in order to cook the wedding feast. But Stumpy could not rest on his laurels. The clan was soon hungry again and he thought it best to teach the men about the atlatl. While this decision was made for the good of the clan, it became his undoing.

Soon, all of the men were bringing in plenty of game. Stumpy showed the clan how to smoke the meat for times when game was scarce. Since all men of the clan could now bring in game, Stumpy's attractiveness suddenly waned. Uma filed for divorce and married Dirk Square Chin.

Stumpy remained loyal to the clan and continued to devise ways of making life easier for them. The clan proved to be ungrateful and treated him shabbily. After learning all he had to offer, they packed up and left while he was away studying plants that had healing powers. The final part of the painting shows Stumpy standing alone staring at the fading footprints of the clan.

And so, it's been throughout history that the short have either been mistreated or insulted by the tall. Even Alexander the Great (who was quite short) was the recipient of disrespect because of his height. There is a famous incident where an ambassador, who had never met the conqueror, knelt before Alexander's second in command because he was the tallest man in the room. Alexander grew so angry that he killed the man on the spot.

There are some who would attribute this killing to the "short man's complex" but nothing could be further from the truth. Alexander, like Stumpy before him, had always been mistreated by taller people. The only reason he wasn't constantly being beaten up was that he was the son of King Philip. The fact that his mom's boyfriends were assassins and snake handlers in a constant state of prancing frenzy probably also kept the bullies away. It took years of hard work to conquer the world and gain worldwide renown. Then some lackey thoughtlessly ignores him because of his height? It is no wonder that Alexander snapped.

A study of the Roman Empire reveals the effect of height-bias on civilization. The Romans were the shortest people in Europe and were pushed around by the Etruscans until they decided to fight back. With brains and discipline this vertically challenged people conquered and civilized the known world. The resulting Pax Romana meant that everyone could enjoy the fruits of the empire. Unfortunately for the world, the tall man's complex brought an end to the Roman Peace.

The Romans granted citizenship to an increasing number of tribes as a reward for their service. Many of these new citizens were taller and as they rose to positions of increasing power, they began to wonder why these short guys were ruling the world. They resented this. They changed the military drastically by requiring that all legionaries be at least six foot tall. This naturally eliminated most of the true Romans from serving in the military. The taller non-Roman legions then allowed their equally tall friends the Huns, Vandals, and others to destroy the empire.

What is it about the short that mankind dislikes? Even as children we are conditioned to think that short is bad and tall is good when we go to our first carnival and are confronted with "You Must Be This Tall to Enter" signs everywhere.

I try to think of movies or TV shows where a leading or major character is short. The list of diminutive leading men is pathetically short; no pun intended. We have Tom Cruise, Robert Redford, Dudley Moore, and Danny Devito to represent the short in the movies. On the TV we have Danny Devito (again) and Tatu. I have had it up to here with "Boss! The plane!" comments. Before anyone tells me I missed a couple of major stars who are short, let me make this clear: Chucky and Yoda are not people.

The short are underrepresented everywhere from business to sports. The only short singers I can think of are Sammy Davis Jr. who's dead and Davey Jones who sang for The Monkees. I suppose we're represented well in jockeys and place kickers. The only area you find short guys in abundance is in the world of geeks.

The reason there are so many short geeks on the planet is simply a matter of survival. Just like Stumpy, they need to use their brains in order to compete with the tall in every aspect of life, especially in the area of procreation. It isn't difficult to see that short guys are at a disadvantage when it comes to finding a mate. One only has to look at the personal ads in any paper to realize that the short are not wanted. Fully two-thirds of all women will list their first preference as men who are at least five feet ten inches or taller. The other third will list height as their second requirement. This means that short guys have to really use their brains to either catch a mate or build one in their basements.

Now some people may ask, "What about short girls? Don't they have the same problems?" With the exception of having to shop in the teen section for clothes, I don't think so. Heck, even short girls don't want short guys. Even in heels they barely reach the chests of their knuckle-dragging boyfriends. My own daughter who is four feet ten married a guy who is six one. How's that for loyalty?

The shabby treatment of the short used to make me angry. Up until I was in my mid-twenties, I believed that the short should receive minority status complete with reparations for the countless centuries of abuse we received at the hands of the tall. A kind of affirmative action for the short would make things right.

I felt that I had a right to fame, fortune, and a hot chick. Because the tall discriminated against the short, they should make it up to me. I should get the job and car that I want. Women should be required to fall in love with me first, other short guys next, then fat guys, ugly guys, poor guys, smelly guys, and tall guys last. It should be a law.

Then I met Mai; beautiful, perfect Mai. She was the most amazing creature to grace the Earth. I asked her out and, to my amazement, she said yes. I took her to an exclusive jazz club. We had a table right in front to see Brian Auger's Oblivion Express. It was going to be my lucky night.

All eyes were on us as we walked in. Mai looked around and then asked, "Where's the DJ?" I told her this was a live music club. She pointed out that there was no dance floor. I told her that people came here to *listen* to music. She wanted to go to a disco. I then realized that this beautiful creature that so bewitched me was a living, breathing rock. She was as dumb as a post. I called her a cab and stayed to listen to the band. I was a bit bummed at first, but I soon forgot Mai because the music was first rate. Another thing that helped me forget was the lovely girl who came to sit with me. She was really impressed that I dumped a beautiful woman for music. So even though the evening started out badly, I wound up having a great time.

There's a pile of lessons I learned that night about life that I could talk about for at least a minute or two. The most obvious lesson was that objects of desire aren't always desirable. Another lesson was that not only was I able to land *and* dump a shallow woman, I could also meet a woman with some depth. My height really doesn't matter to people with substance.

I've learned that everyone on the planet has a reason to complain. We all feel slighted because of our race, language, religion, disability, even our height. There is no law or program that will ever change how we feel about ourselves or others around us. I only know that I can change some things and some things I learn to accept. I'll always envy some people and, yet I know that there are some people who are envious of me. I have been fortunate enough to become a father and grandfather. I've traveled the world and have seen a lot. I think I've received a pretty fair shake in life and that's fine with me.

Now all of this is fine and good. But whatever became of Stumpy? I'm pleased to inform you that Stumpy did not die alone. In fact, he did quite well for himself. After wandering for a few years, he wound up in the Middle East where he created agriculture, married, and fathered many children. One of his descendants, Stumparabi, founded Sumer and sent his grandson Stumpmosis IV to establish the first Egyptian dynasty.

My research into Stumpy's life proves to me that there really isn't a short man's complex just the mistaken perception of the tall due to their own envy of the short. It also proves the Rolling Stones were right when they sang, "You can't always get what you want. But if you try some time, you might find you get what you need." And this brings me to another song and songwriter that I really need to discuss things with.

KING KONG – A LESSON IN CRITICAL THINKING

I've read that critical thinking is the mental process of actively and skillfully conceptualizing, applying, analyzing, synthesizing, and evaluating information to reach an answer or conclusion. Contrary to popular belief, the definition does not mean criticizing that with which one does not agree. Stating that someone with a differing opinion is stupid or visually repugnant maybe critical and quite possibly true but it has nothing to do with thinking since it has nothing to do with the issue in question.

The only people who regularly practice critical thinking are little kids because they are curious by nature and not always accepting of explanations. We lose our ability to think critically once we reach puberty because of our innate desire to be accepted. Our curiosity is stifled by the scornful looks of adults whenever we ask, "Why?" We learn to stop questioning things when everyone we know has stopped asking questions. With the death of curiosity, we no longer actively practice critical thinking because we have ceased to believe in its importance.

As I try to remember my own exercises in critical thinking I think back to when I was six and how I disagreed with the conclusions of some scientists while watching a documentary during the Saturday Matinee on Channel 12. These scientist guys back in 1933 discovered an uncharted island inhabited by a previously unknown tribe. This tribe never bothered anyone except for the occasional native who would be tied to a stick and eaten by a giant ape name Kong. The scientists thought the natives worshipped Kong and sacrificed people to him, so he wouldn't destroy their village. Even at that young age, I knew the scientists were wrong. I had observed that the island was full of other giant animals and dinosaurs. Kong was always fighting them and protecting the tribe. The tribesmen rewarded him for that protection by giving him a daily snack on a stick with a big bowl of gravy.

The scientists had come to the island with a blonde lady scientist named Fay Wray. I didn't know why these supposedly smart guys would've brought her because she was pretty useless on the expedition. I think she earned her doctorate in screaming at big animals and falling down with a twisted ankle at the worst possible moment. She was as dumb as a post. Now that I'm older, I realize she was brought along because she smelled nice.

When the scientists arrived, they were welcomed warmly by the natives. The stupid scientists thought to themselves they think we're great

White gods! They were wrong. The natives actually thought that Kong might like some American food for a change and promptly tied the useless, screaming blonde scientist to a shish kabob stick and rang the dinner bell.

As luck would have it, Kong had just finished fighting a T-Rex and he was famished so he came rushing to see what Chef Francois Wakawaka had prepared for an appetizer. He grabbed the screaming blonde who was screaming her blonde head off. He looked at her. He looked around and roared like crazy. The stupid scientists thought he was mad that a beautiful blonde could be mistreated, and he wanted to save her. They were once again wrong.

What they failed to notice was that Chef Francois had forgotten to fill the gravy bowl. Kong looked at his food and then at the empty gravy bowl. In Giant Ape-ese he roared, "What! No gravy?!!!" He busted down the gate roaring, "Gravy! I want gravy!"

I mention this documentary because not only does it demonstrate how a lack of critical thinking almost resulted in the destruction of New York City leading to the supposed demise of a unique zoological specimen, it also marks the first time I consciously questioned conventional thought. After all, why would the natives build a giant gate to keep Kong out if he had hands that could open the gate? Didn't they build it to keep out the really dangerous creatures? Why would they think of the scientists as gods if they fed the blonde one to Kong? Why would Kong fall in love with a screaming blonde? Heck, screaming blondes can be pretty darned annoying to humans much less a giant ape.

There are some who may say the questions and observations of a child have nothing to do with critical thinking. To those people I reply, "Oh, ye of little brain! Questions and observations are at the very heart of critical thinking." I learned that from a speech given by the late Congressman Henry B. Gonzales in 1969 at Brentwood Junior High. He was kind of a godlike figure in San Antonio back then. Almost every household in the West and South Side of town had pictures of La Virgen de Guadalupe, the Pope, and John F. Kennedy hanging next to a Henry B. calendar. He visited my school to talk to us about citizenship.

Godlike figure or not, any lecture or speech given by anyone is pretty much a death sentence to a bunch of 7th and 8th graders. In fact, it's a death sentence to any kid prior to graduation. During most of that one-hour ordeal all I heard in between the occasional fart and laugher was, "Blah, blah, blah," and "Yadda, yadda, yadda." Every once in a while, I would actually pick up a comment I could understand like, "Your teachers are not here to help you become happy and successful. They are here to teach you to become productive citizens." That comment sort of woke me from my slack-jawed stupor long enough hear him say that we owed it to ourselves to think for ourselves whenever making decisions. I remember him saying, "Don't always believe everything you read and hear because it may be wrong. If you have a question, ask it. If you get no answer, then find it yourself." When someone asked him how we should vote, Congressman Gonzales said, "I can't tell you how to vote. No one can do that. When you're old enough to vote you have to figure out who's the best man for the job and then vote for him." Once I turned eighteen, I voted for Henry B. every two years until the end.

Anyone thinking that my loyalty to the congressman stemmed solely from the fact that I liked him would be wrong. I voted for him because he did a good job, he was honest, and courageous. I didn't always agree with him but his actions showed a great love for San Antonio and the United States. He also had a big nose that reminded me of my grandfather's big nose... really.

I was constantly reminded of Henry B's admonition against believing everything I heard or read each time I saw a new documentary, especially where Japanese scientists were concerned. They obviously didn't know how to properly destroy monsters since there seemed to be an endless supply of Godzillas destroying Tokyo every other month. I'll say this much, I don't think we Americans could rebuild New York as quickly and as many times as Tokyo's been rebuilt. Then again, I think New Yorkers would have the good sense to move elsewhere the third time they saw a Japanese documentary crew arrive in town.

While curiosity and disbelief are often the impetus for critical thinking, defending one's own beliefs can lead to the practice as well. There was this guy I knew who had a thing against Catholics and the Catholic Church. He constantly attacked the Church and its history. Any time someone tried to defend the Church, he would say something like "you need to hold a mirror up to yourselves. You might not like what you see."

One day, he starts talking about how the Church kept Europe in the Dark Ages because it forced everyone to speak and read in Latin and the people didn't understand Latin because they were poor and couldn't afford to learn it and the priests would have fun with the ignorant parishioners by singing Stand Upo En Kneelo Downo! Then the stupid peasants would sing Amen! Well it sounded plausible enough to me and I thought to myself maybe he's right about us. Maybe I should look in the mirror. Hey! Look at me! I'm pretty freaking handsome! Hey, wait a minute! I've actually read a book or two and what was that thing I remember about the Roman Empire?

"Hey, Professor Sani-Flush," I said to the guy, "I think Europe was pretty much conquered by the Romans who, if I recall correctly, spoke Latin and held all trade in Latin and taught the natives Latin and anyone who traveled around needed to know Latin because it was understood by nearly everyone which made it a truly international language and that was before the rise of the Catholic Church which merely utilized the language understood by most people because without a printing press, books had to be handwritten by monks with cramped hands who didn't like writing things more than once and so wrote in Latin so the books could be passed around the known world spreading a message of love and understanding in Latin so I think you'd better give me three mea culpas before I beat you with this St. Christopher I'm holding." Okay, I didn't really threaten him, but he did back off and muttered something like, "but... church... bad... uh... not good... uh..."

Speaking of religion, I'd say the Devil's Advocate plays a huge role in the area of critical thinking. I remember a teacher who divided us into opposing teams to debate an issue. We had two days to get ready for the debate. Two days later we were told that our teams had to switch sides and prepare for the real debate where we had to argue the other team's point and they had to argue ours. The winning team would get extra credit. It was tough, but that exercise taught me that I should always consider every aspect of an issue if I ever wanted to come to a sound decision.

One guy who was really adept at seeing both sides of an issue was the Catholic theologian, Thomas Aquinas. I know there are some who think I should pronounce the name as "Ah-kEE-nahs" but I saw The Name of the Rose starring Sean Connery where he plays a monk back in the Middle Ages who's investigating the mysterious deaths of some other monks. Well, he pronounced the name as "tOm-ish uh-kwEYE-nish" and since I wouldn't dare contradict James Bond wearing a habit and exploding sandals, I'll stick with his pronunciation but it's hard to talk like him and say, "tOm-ish uh-kwEYE-nish" I'll just stick with Thomas Aquinas.

Anyway, Aquinas had a big problem because he was smart. He was also a Catholic which meant that he had to write a lot of stuff for the Church which kept him supplied with some pretty good wine. It turned out there some guys called "heretics" who used to say bad stuff about the

Church and even about God Himself. The Pope called Thomas over and asked him to respond to the attacks. So, armed with a stack of paper, a couple of cases of wine, and all the government cheese he could eat, Thomas came up with what I think is the greatest work of theology, the "Summa Theologica" which presented the prevailing arguments both for and against the teachings of the Church. The brilliance of this work was that Aquinas really studied his opposition and presented their arguments as strongly as if he were one of them. By truly understanding the heretics' views he was better able to present a counter argument. Anyone who thinks he used lame heretical arguments, so he could squash them with superior religious dogma needs to read the argument on the existence of God where on the one hand he proves convincingly that God does not exist and on the other hand proves his existence with a discussion on the Law of Motion. The reader is quite free to choose what to believe.

Now that I think about it, maybe Thomas Aquinas was one of those split personality types. Maybe he didn't have any friends and took to holding conversations with himself. I wonder if he got into shouting matches with himself at the monastery. I can imagine the monks in training staying clear of the weird, mumbling guy. Well, mumbling guy or not, he taught me that I should not only know what the heck I'm talking about but also what the heck the other guy's talking about before I start dismissing his view because he may have a point which brings to mind probably the single most important aspect of critical thinking that is glaring in its absence from today's so-called thinkers: Respect for a worthy opponent.

General Patton was a guy who knew about respect and he'd slap the teeth right out of your head to make sure you knew about it too. His opponent in WW II was the great German general Rommel. The two generals had great respect for one other. Yeah, they wanted to kill each other as well but in a respectful manner. Rommel was a tactical genius and wrote a book on tactics. Patton wasn't as brilliant as Rommel, but he was smarter because he studied Rommel's tactics. There was one battle where Patton poked Rommel's forces in the eye. After the battle, Patton famously yelled, "Rommel, you magnificent bastard! I read your book!" Okay, that line came from a movie about Patton, but I still love that line. I always wanted to have the opportunity to greet a worthy opponent with a hearty, "you magnificent bastard!" with respect, of course.

Lack of respect is really a lack of critical thinking which brings me to what I was talking about earlier. The scientist guys didn't respect Kong. They didn't care about him. Look! He's a big monkey! Look! He loves the screaming blonde! Look! We are superior to him and he will be our pet!

Kong was the one who showed he could think critically. He wanted to eat the blonde, but he didn't have any gravy. He let the scientist guys take him to America because he heard it was the Land of Milk and Gravy. He thought he'd cooperate with the humans in the hope of getting some gravy and that's the only reason he let them chain him up on the stage. Kong was a bit embarrassed since he wasn't wearing any pants, but he took it in stride until the cameras started flashing. He thought, Mom's gonna kill me if she sees these pictures on the internet! He naturally went berserk. Who can blame any giant ape for stomping on the paparazzi? He also figured out that it wasn't a good idea to eat the screaming blonde since there were military guys shooting at him and it hurt like heck.

Well Kong was no fool. He didn't want to die so he struck a deal with a movie guy and faked his death using one of the life-sized King Kong souvenir dolls they sell on Skull Island. Kong went on to star in some films over the years and earned enough money to keep him in gravy and hot giant ape chicks for the rest of his life.

I'm fully aware that some of my audience may not believe a word of what I've just said and that's okay. There are some who may want to verify the facts as I've presented them and that's okay. Reaction to any information shows interest. Interest leads to curiosity. Curiosity leads to questions and having questions is the spark that ignites critical thinking.

I'm reminded of a saying that I used to see on t-shirts and bumper stickers - QUESTION AUTHORITY. I wonder if it was an order. I wonder why I've stopped seeing them around 2009. I can imagine the guy who made up that slogan suddenly taking over the world and telling us all, "Remember when I told you to question authority? Well you can stop now."

I have some questions for that guy.

SOMETHING TO THINK ABOUT

Hi. I was born a few years ago. My given name is Gilbert Joseph Polanco. A few months ago, I signed a contract with a book publisher. I'm still broke so I'm not quitting my day job any time soon. I was given the privilege of speaking before you for a number of possible reasons: 1) I wrote a book; 2) I'm Brown; 3) I'm so handsome it's scary; 4) Everything I say is fascinating or 5) the speaker they really wanted wasn't available.

Whatever the reason, I'm here to say something… Hispanic. More accurately, I'm here to say something that is suitable for the celebration of Hispanic Heritage Month. There are some who hate the term "Hispanic" for various reasons, but that issue is something best left for others to argue. To me, it's just another word that's been used to describe me like Mexican, Mexican-American, Spanish, Latin, Latino, Chicano, American, Mijo, Dad, Grandpa, drummer, artist, curioso, baboso, chaparro, and stud muffin. As you can see, I am not only painfully good looking but also a man of great diversity and therefore hard to describe in 20 or 30 minutes. It's a heck of a lot more difficult to define and understand the group known as Hispanics which is comprised of countless individuals and cultures.

There are many who have and will tell you about who you are, what you are, and where you came from. You will listen to them because they are educated and obviously know more than you. I'm not that guy because I've only studied that which is meaningful to me in the quest to learn about my ancestors and ultimately about myself. The more I learn, the more I realize how ignorant I am. I really can only tell you about my history. I can only hope that you may want to start learning your own history. Understanding history is important because who we are today is a result of who we were in the past.

The secret to learning anything starts with curiosity which leads to asking questions. After getting unsatisfactory answers, you must research, interpret and finally analyze data. In other words, you gotta figure it out yourself. My first experience with real learning came when I saw the movie El Cid. I asked a teacher about him and she suggested I go do some research. Researching anything was tough when I was young. We didn't have the internet or cable TV. To find out anything at all, I had to visit a building that was known as a "library" and read things that were known as "books."

I learned that El Cid's name was Rodrigo Diaz and he is the national hero of Spain. I read the epic poem about him. I found passages about him in the encyclopedia and other books. I learned that he liberated

Valencia from Muslim occupation in 1099 about 380 years after they conquered and occupied southern Spain. I should probably point out that my learning about the Islamic conquest of European lands almost 400 years before the First Crusade wound up causing a heated debate between me and one of my history teachers.

It was and is a thrill to learn stuff that my teachers couldn't or wouldn't teach and if they did touch on subjects I had studied on my own, I was able to form my own opinions before they formed them for me. Such is the case with the Alamo. I was taught that the battle was fought between Texans and Mexicans. During a visit to the Alamo, I read the list of the defenders who died there. There were a few names of these Texas heroes who could've been Mexican. I wondered who these guys were and learned that they were indeed Mexicans. They didn't call themselves Mexican. They called themselves Tejanos. The White Texans didn't call themselves Texans. They called themselves Texians. It came as a shock that only six of the Alamo's defenders who died were actually born in Texas. All six of them were Tejanos.

One of the six Tejanos who died in the battle was Gregorio Esparza. His brother, Francisco, served under General Cos so this made for a brother against brother story. Francisco was allowed to recover Gregorio's body and give him a proper burial while the rest of the Alamo defenders were buried in a mass grave. There is a disputed story that Santa Ana supposedly told Gregorio's grieving mother that the reason he allowed her son to be buried was that at least one her sons was a good Mexican. Now that story really bugged me. It's often been a cause of arguments on one side or the other.

As I thought about it, I realized that there are more than two sides to every story. Whether the story is true or false is immaterial. You see, we only hear a Mexican or Texan side of the story and the Tejanos are completely ignored. Since there were so few references to Tejanos I tried to understand them by pretending I lived back then in order to get a glimpse of who they were. The Tejanos really got the shaft from both sides of the fence and there are some who wonder why they fought against Mexico. It really came down basics. The Tejanos lived here. This was their home and they defended it. I also thought about Esparza's mother and what she must have felt having sons on opposite sides. If Santa Ana had indeed said what is attributed to him, I would like to think that she would have stood proud, looked the general in the eye and said, "Yes, I have a son that is a good Mexican. My other son who lies before you was a good Tejano."

That thought led me to try to learn more about Texas history because, after all this is my home. The Polanco family has been in Texas since the 1800's. Although my family name isn't very common, I've found that there are a pile of Polanco's everywhere. There was a Francisco Polanco who was the secretary for Saint Ignacious and was close to becoming the Pope until his brother was accused of being a Jew. There was another who was tried by the Inquisition in Mexico. There was a Polanco who was an officer under Pancho Villa and still another who was hung by him. There is the Blessed Anselmo Polanco and then there is Gaspar Polanco who was the first Polanco to set foot in the New World. This Polanco was a Spaniard in Cortez' army that, with the help of the Tlaxcala, ravaged the Mexica nation and eventually led to the destruction of much of our indigenous history.

It's enlightening for me to learn my family history but, sadly, it's much easier to trace the Spanish side than the native side. I used to like to think of my native side to be Azteca, but the more I research, the more it looks like my indigenous roots are Maya. Someday I plan to spend the money to trace my bloodline through a DNA project I read about. I may find out I'm actually Polynesian and there's a whole other story in that.

In the process of learning stuff, I started noticing that things people (ourselves included) believe can be downright goofy. There was this guy who was talking about the Popol Vuh and how this Mayan "Book of the Dead" predicted the end of the world in 2012. Well the guy obviously hadn't read it because he would have known it as the Quiche Book of Creation. There was also Eric von Donikan who famously claimed that the carving on the sarcophagus lid of an "unknown" Mayan king was a depiction of a man in a space ship. Of course, the "unknown" Mayan king is actually Pacal and the carving depicts his descent into the jaws of the underworld which is Xibalba.

I can't stress enough the importance of reading and truly learning everything you can about yourself, your history, and your heritage. There are far too many people who think that watching The Discovery Channel or seeing the movie Apocalypto makes them knowledgeable in indigenous culture. I'm waiting to meet a cool Chicano artist with Mayan glyph tattoos on his arm and wearing a Che Guevara t-shirt. When asked the meaning of the glyphs, the cool artist coolly responds, "It is the symbol for Ma'kal in kaal who was the Mayan king from which my family descends." As I walk away, I can only think that "my throat is sore" is a strange name for a king.

Now I've talked about a whole pile of stuff regarding things I've learned. Two of the most important things I learned are that there are very few people who know everything about anything and the people who do know everything are probably wrong.

Read a bunch of stuff. It's really fun when you don't have to do it. Read Stolen Continents by Ronald Wright, The Popo Vuh, Maya Script by Maria Longhena, The History of the Indies of New Spain by Fray Diego Duran, The Early Spanish Main by Carl Ortwin Sauer, Montezuma by C.A. Burland, A Forest of Kings by Linda Schele & David Freidel, The Conquest of New Spain by Bernal Diaz, Cabeza de Vaca's report to the King of Spain, Sahagun's work on the Mexica, and countless others.

Try to learn about Pacal, Lady Evening Star, Nazhual Coyotl, Cuatemoc, Yax Balam, Gregorio Cortez, Juan Seguin and the Tejanos. Ask yourselves, "Who was Malinche?" What is the true native language of Mexico? Is anyone puro Mexicano? What the heck is Hispanic anyway? Are we all Brown? Why don't we all speak Spanish? Where do we come from? Why did the Tlaxcala help Cortez? How many cultures and languages comprise the group known as Hispanics? Do all Hispanics think alike? Is this guy ever going to shut up?

Yeah, I know I just blew through a whole slew of topics and haven't even scratched the surface of Hispanic history and culture. I can't tell you everything you need to know about anything. That's something only you can do. When you truly start learning, you'll find that several people looking at the same thing will come upon several different conclusions about that thing. Be open to everything. Be open to the fact that you may actually know something a more educated person does not. Be open to the fact that your conclusions may be wrong. You need to learn how to think before anyone can tell you what to think.

If I have learned anything in life, it's that of all the things I am or was, I am first and foremost a human being and I still have a lot to learn.

THE SUIT

Good evening everyone.

We are gathered here to celebrate the accomplishments of an elite group of people. I'm not talking about the Navy Seals or the Green Berets. I'm talking about students who have demonstrated a desire to do more than just get by. I'm talking about students who take learning seriously. So, I jumped at the chance when I was offered the honor of speaking before you.

Right after jumping at that chance, I jumped into my closet to look for the one suit that I own which hasn't been worn in eight or nine years. After knocking off the dust I noticed, that while the suit hadn't changed at all, I had changed a lot… I think by a good three inches. I looked in the mirror. I then looked at the dust that was still settling after I had shaken the suit and thought to myself that there was something to be learned from the image of a dusty, ill-fitting suit that I could pass on to you. You may be wondering *what in the heck does an old suit have to do with being inducted tonight?* The answer is simple. It provides a visual demonstration of potential and actualization.

Looking at the society's website I found that, *"The purpose of Phi Theta Kappa shall be to recognize and encourage scholarship among two-year college students. To achieve this purpose, Phi Theta Kappa shall provide opportunity for the development of leadership and service, for an intellectual climate for exchange of ideas and ideals, for lively fellowship for scholars, and for stimulation of interest in continuing academic excellence."*

In other words, through your own work you've shown the potential to become an asset to society. You are now being given help in realizing that potential. Now I know that some of you are probably thinking, *yeah, but what about the suit? Tell me about the suit!*

This suit, like a diploma, a membership card, or a badge is nothing but an inanimate object. All it does on its own is hang around and be a suit. It waits for someone to give it meaning. It waits for someone to give it purpose.

As a young man, I hated suits. Some people might think that that I hated them because I was a long haired hippy freak who was rebelling against "The Establishment." Actually, I was long haired hippy freak who thought that suits just weren't cool. After all, what could be cooler than me? I was born naturally handsome with a brilliant mind. I know this because my mother told me so.

I was cursed with the natural ability to do almost anything without trying very hard. School was a snap. I could pass any class with my eyes closed. In fact, my eyes were closed a lot during class. I wrote the term papers for half of my classmates. I had teachers and professors tell me that I needed to be a writer. I was offered help in that regard many times. I passed up those offers because I was too busy experiencing Life knowing that I could always *do it later*... Later never came. I did not become a recording artist. I did not become a professional writer. I did not do a lot. The only thing I really did do was read and read and read and think about what I was *going to do someday*.

When I retired from the Navy, I realized I needed to get a job. To get a job, I needed a suit. This suit in fact. I looked good enough in it to fool people into thinking that I was of a professional bent. After getting the job, I wore the suit a few more times and then put it away to gather dust.

I'm not sure when it happened but a voice deep inside me spoke and said, "Gilbert. Do something." So, I did. I worked on my drumming and most especially my writing. Over the past few years I've recorded with several artists on five CDs and there are two new projects in the works. The writing has been a little tougher, but I finally finished my first book and after making some mistakes as a new writer, I learned there are people who can support and help me with my next project. Another thing that I learned is that I can't succeed on my dashing good looks and incredible talent alone. I actually have to *do something* with my ability. Without doing, potential means nothing.

Every one of you has already actualized some of your potential. You did that through hard work and study. There is a huge difference between people who go to school and people who get an education. The fact that you have maintained a 3.5 cumulative average tells me that you care about learning and you are in fact getting an education.

Anyone looking at your record will immediately see the potential within you. Phi Theta Kappa has seen that potential as well. You now have a support group that can help you access the tools you will need to not only increase your potential but to actualize it as well. You have every right to feel proud tonight. You have earned congratulations for *earning* membership into a group that is open to only a select few.

I'd like to remind you though that whatever level of education you achieve, the diploma that will hang on your wall does only one thing. It tells people that you know stuff. That's all. It's what you do with that stuff that's important.

The late Henry B. Gonzales once told me that school didn't exist to make me happy. It existed to help me become a useful and productive member of society. He explained that we owe it to ourselves and society to contribute our talents and abilities in any way we can.

If we don't contribute to society, we not only fail to realize our potential, we risk the shame becoming useless like an old dusty suit hanging forgotten in a closet for eight or nine years. Yeah, I haven't forgotten the suit. Heck, I'm wearing it.

This suit once made me look pretty snazzy. As I looked at it after dusting it off I thought it could potentially make me look pretty snazzy again. Imagine my disappointment when I looked in the mirror.

Is this the actualization of the suit's potential? I think not. You see, after I actually started *doing* things I learned that I can change things around me. I have something else I can work on and change. I'm going to work on my physical fitness and make this suit look good on me again.

I imagine we all have our own mental dusty suits we haven't tried on in a while. Heck, take them out. Put them on. Make them fit. Go out in the world. Be appreciative when people come up to you and say, "Hey! Nice suit!" Of course, that suit can be any number of things that you do from writing a poem to curing cancer.

After all, when we eventually leave this world, the only thing people will remember is what we did. Now that reminds me of a movie about an old bluesman talking to a kid. He said, "When all is said and done, the only thing you can hope for is for someone to remember you and say, man he could really play."

My hope for you is to do and to be remembered for the things that you do. Then you will realize the actualization of your potential. As for me, I'm going to get working on fitting into this suit right again. Then again, I just might buy me a new suit.

Once again, congratulations on your achievements.

Thank you and good night.

The Reformed Revolutionary

I was intrigued by the conference's theme, "Reform or Revolution" because I'm a revolutionary at heart and I'm constantly reforming my ways. As a kid, I was always rebelling against one thing or another, especially when it came to eating my vegetables. To a five-year-old revolutionary, veggies are a means of oppression inflicted on the young by the greedy dictators known as "Parents" who keep all the ice cream and chocolate milk for themselves denying him the tasty delicacies that are rightfully his by virtue of his existence.

Of course, as I grew older, my predilection for revolution became a little more refined. I learned that out and out rebellion would often lead to me being sent to my room. On very rare occasions, the ultimate punishment was given: The Lecture. The Lecture was normally administered by Dad who would often preface this torture with, "Your Mother is very disappointed with you."

Now there are some who may believe that I am not taking the idea of reform or revolution seriously. After all, what does my experience as an ice cream-crazed kid have to do with the question of correcting injustice? To answer that, we have to define "injustice." We must ask ourselves if one's perception of injustice is the same as another's? Do the perceptions of all rational beings warrant equal study? Is an ice cream-crazed kid a rational being? Heck, that's a lot of stuff to think about before one can even begin to contemplate the reformation of or revolting against an institution that may or may not be worth keeping. After two or three minutes of careful contemplation, my solution to answering this problem is "dyeeeee" which is what I came up with after realizing there are about eight billion opinions on the matter.

I guess the only thing I can relay to anyone with a degree of certainty is my own opinion. Contrary to popular belief, I didn't pull this opinion from my como se llama. Some things I learned from history, some from observation, and some things I learned by stepping in a pile of crap. After stepping in enough crap, I learned to clean it up or avoid it altogether. Sometimes you can turn it into fertilizer. Sometimes you just wallow in it, but I wouldn't want to do that because then I'd become a politician.

Since I wasn't a politician but rather a young revolutionary in training without direction or a mentor, I had to learn things on my own. The lessons I learned were often confusing and seemingly contradictory. Take for example, my big brother who was always working at one thing or another to make money. Every once in a while, he'd buy me a Big Red or ice cream from his own money. There were plenty of times he didn't and when he didn't I would cry. If I cried hard enough, Eddie would be ordered by the authorities to share the wealth that he earned with the unfortunate sibling who didn't work.

That worked out pretty well until I turned ten. I don't remember exactly how it happened, but Eddie came home eating some ice cream and wouldn't give me any. I immediately started crying. Dad pulled me aside and told me I wasn't a baby and to quit my bawling. He told me that Eddie always earned his money and shared whenever he could. "But it's not fair! He has ice cream and I don't!" I cried. "Your brother worked hard for that money and it's not fair to take it from him just because you want it. That's stealing." I was flabbergasted.

I was further shocked when Dad pointed to our yard and our ancient push mower. "You want ice cream? You're going to have to earn it." Now I don't know if you know what a push mower is but back in the sixties, about half the country used these things to cut the grass. They didn't do such a good job. I had to go over the lawn two or three times, follow it up with the weed whacker which was a medieval device that looked kind of like a hand saw attached to a broom stick that would cut down any living thing in its path. That, my friends, is green technology. The only fouling of the air would've been my language if I only knew how to cuss back then. I would've given anything for a gas mower and now that I have one, I'm not giving it up. If you want my mower, you're going to have to pry it from my cold, dead hands!

But what does this have to do with being a revolutionary? Everything, actually. I learned early on that you can't revolt against something you don't care about. Well, nowadays, that may not be so true since so many people think it's a cool thing. I once saw an ad that read, "Rich, successful parents got you down? Then buy a Che Guevarra t-shirt." What a cool guy. I remember as a kid, my Dad told me, "he looks like Cantiflas with a gun, only he's not as funny." Like most kids, I read the popular stuff about him, but I also read enough about his dealing with the vanquished to know he wasn't so cool.

What was cool though was reading. I was and still am all sorts of stupid over reading. I really go goofy with history. I've always thought that history was so much cooler than movies because the stories were so much better. I kid you not. Spend some time reading Tacitus and you'll know that the most graphic, crazy, and violent flicks are mere bedtime stories compared to stuff that really happened. There wasn't much revolting back then, just a bunch of conquering. People think we're living in bad times. Read Herodotus. If you were an ordinary Joe back then, your life really sucked. Life really, really sucked all over the world for a heck of a long time.

One day, you could be sitting around, eating grapes, waiting for your useless wife to slaughter and cook the family pig before refilling the cups of your friends Flatus and Testikles and suddenly Cyrus the Great is knocking on your door. The next thing you know, you and your buddies are turned into eunuchs and made to guard your wives who have been placed in the harem of Cyrus the Great. It kind of puts things in perspective.

You wouldn't be fighting for your rights back then because the only people with rights were the guys with swords and axes. I don't think that anyone really thought about rights until the Magna Carta was written. Yeah, I know that a bunch of sandal and bed sheet wearing guys in Athens came up with democracy and the Romans had a republic but until a couple of hundred years ago, most people still had deal with guys sticking sharp objects in them and feeding them to lions and stuff.

Well, stuff started changing when folks began to keep their own stuff because a few aristocrats had the brains to realize that it was a lot easier to govern if people were happy. Ownership meant investment which led to prosperity. By allowing people to prosper it was easier to defend the realm against conquerors because instead of having a few thousand guys to defend the land at a huge cost, there was a whole pile of guys with pitchforks ready to take the field against other guys who wanted to take their stuff. Another advantage of letting people have their own stuff was the reduction in the cost of keeping people happy.

Smart rulers knew that they had to provide the people with holidays and festivals for the country every once in a while. Collecting all the beer and hotdogs throughout the realm and redistributing it to the locals cost a heck of a lot. Heck, the people were already making beer and hotdogs. Why not let them keep it and party how they chose? Cutting out the middle man saved a heck of a lot of money. It also cut out reasons for people to revolt.

But every place in the world didn't have smart guys running the show. Most people had their stuff taken from them. They didn't like that. Probably the most important thing a guy owns is himself. Since the guys who were taking, and enslaving folks were pretty darned strong, there wasn't much anyone could do. Eventually, there comes someone who can do something. The first revolutionary I read about was a guy named Spartacus.

Spartacus was a slave and a gladiator to boot. Gladiators were guys who knew how to fight. They were forced to fight and die in front of the unemployed Roman population to keep them happy, so they could keep the powers that be in power. Well Spartacus was sick of being the entertainment for both the rich and the freeloaders alike, so he started a revolt. No one had ever seen anything like it. Suddenly, the Roman guys with sharp pointy objects were being faced with slaves with sharp pointy objects who knew how to use them. Sadly, while Spartacus knew how to revolt he didn't know what to do after the revolt. Here were piles of guys who revolted with him and faced with the question: What now? Well, lack of planning resulted in crucifixion. That really sucked.

The next revolutionaries I read about were the founders of the United States. Now these pony-tailed guys had no idea that they'd be revolutionaries. They were British citizens who were prospering in the colonies. They didn't begrudge the crown lawful taxes but after a while, they started losing more and more of their stuff and what made things worse, they didn't have a say in where their stuff went. After a while, enough guys got sick of their stuff being taken and redistributed to those bums in England who didn't earn it, so they revolted. They succeeded because they knew exactly why they revolted and made sure that everyone else did as well by writing the Declaration of Independence. They followed it up with a thing called The Constitution and The Bill of Rights. I think that, despite the many failings of their descendants, the American revolutionaries were very successful.

There have been other revolutions. Some have been successful and some not so successful. There was the French Revolution which resulted in lots of heads being chopped off and free berets for everyone. The Russian Revolution was both successful and a tragedy. While redistributing wealth, the Bolsheviks took from the People the one thing that should be the most important: Free Thought. Millions died in the gulags because they didn't agree with The Party or because they wanted to keep their own stuff.

Forcing people to think like you is a very bad thing. The Khmer Rouge revolution in Cambodia is stark proof of that. Being a business owner, a teacher, a musician, a homosexual, or a religious person was enough of a crime to be sent to the killing fields where the number of dead will never be known.

The big problem with revolution is that most people don't think it out. Why in the heck are we revolting? What do we do after the revolt? Too many times, the result is to keep on revolting. After a while there are enough dead people or people in reeducation camps that the only thing to save the people is a revolt against the revolution.

Sometimes it's just better to reform a thing. Our history is full of reforms that have done a lot of good. The Suffrage and Civil Rights Acts are reforms that have done a lot of good. Reform is a less violent way of fixing something that's broke. It's not as glamorous as revolution but there are a lot fewer dead guys to bury.

Before deciding to revolt or reform, people should really look at the problem at hand. Is this machine really broken? Should I take it apart? Should I replace the doodad with a TransFabulator 5000? Maybe I should just read and follow the directions that came in the box.

A good example of this is the question of hate crime law. This topic causes a lot of arguments because it is subjective rather than objective. Why not just make the courts apply the laws as they were written? Say a guy kills another guy and is tried for murder in a death penalty state. He's sentenced to death but since he's also convicted of a hate crime, what are you supposed to do? Hang him twice? Piss on his grave? Come on, Judge! Just follow the damned law. There's a reason why lawyers are the first to be killed in a revolt.

It's important to think before acting. There seems to be a current sentiment that we should revolt against something as nebulous as Greed. Greed is one of the seven deadly sins which to some minds would seem to be a worthy thing to revolt against. But why revolt against Greed? Is the reason for our dissatisfaction Envy? Is not Envy also one of the deadly sins? How about we revolt against Wrath? How about Gluttony? I'm sure people would have a hard time revolting against Pride and Lust. And just how does one revolt against Sloth?

I guess the problem with wannabe revolutionaries nowadays is they live in a pretty good place and are dissatisfied with the stuff they have. They look at someone with more stuff and say, "Hey! I should have that stuff! We are all equal and should have the same things!" While we are all equal in the eyes of God, we are not all equal in the eyes of each other. After all, just because your Mom says you're handsome, it doesn't mean that you're going to get laid.

I guess I'm not the revolutionary I was when I was a kid. I'm just a guy who raised a family, works, plays drums, drinks, cusses, and generally earned the things I have. I have less than some and more than others. What I do have I earned. When I can, I share. Don't take my stuff. It's not yours. If you do try, then you may face a real revolutionary and in that Spirit of Revolution, I present for you:

SOUFFLE FOR THE MASSES

There was a man who was a manly man.
Who cooked soufflés in the zoo
He liked to use cheetah milk
And an ostrich egg or two
The tourists, they chased him
With forks and bats and knives
They were led by the Hungarian Merchant
And his seven hideous wives

What is this he thought
What is this he cried
As he whipped the ostrich eggs
In the bowl of steaming cheetah milk
Between Sophia's legs

They occupied the once clean zoo
Singing songs and spraying paint
On the manly man and Sophia
Who asked, "What is your complaint?"
"We want soufflés!" screamed the Ninety-Nine
As they chased them round the block
But their sense was only six per cent
Of a gibbon and a rock

What is this he thought?
What is this he cried?
As they stopped and scratched their chins
We don't know, and we don't care
But you're guilty of some sin

The manly man took Sophia
To the cage of the Stupid Beast
They set him loose upon the crowd
They were a tasty feast
When all were gone they cooked soufflés
And were joined by the working few
Who brought all their own produce
And a keg of beer or two

What is this he thought
What is this he cried
As they hugged him in their turn
We don't know, and we don't care
But you get just what you earned

YOU PEOPLE

A few years ago, I went to Sam's Burger Joint to see my friend Eric Hisaw perform his songs for the dinner crowd. Sam's is located north of downtown San Antonio on Broadway. I've performed there with different bands over the years and I really like the place.

It was pretty packed that day and I shared a table with my friend, Terry, his girlfriend, and a young lady name Andrea who had nowhere to sit. Eric was playing and singing, and we were all having a good time. As is the case whenever I drink responsibly, I had the sudden urge to check out the décor of the establishment's restroom.

As I walked down the hall to my destination, I noticed a young woman trying to enter the women's restroom. She was furiously turning the knob and pounding on the door. "Bladquit maddaflippa!" she screamed along with some other choice words I didn't understand.

She probably had to go pretty bad, so I checked the men's room. It was empty and kind of clean. I figured she could go in there while I stood watch. I opened the door and called to her, "Hey, this one's empty!" as I pointed inside.

She spun around with blinding speed, flung out her arm, and in her hand, was a little bird which she pointed at me as she screamed, "Sploink you and your sploinking penis!" Her chest was heaving and there was murder in her eyes. I was flabbergasted. *Sploink me and my sploinking penis?*

"Suit yourself," I said as I went in to do my business. I put the crazed woman out of my mind.

I got back to my table and then remembered that I hadn't given Terry a copy of my book.

Commercial interruption – Did I forget to mention that I wrote a book? It's called FOR REALS! OBSERVATIONS BY A BROWN GUY and it's available on the internet for only forty-nine ninety-nine ninety-five or you can meet me on the corner of Marbach & Pinn Rd at 5:30 and get some copies for dozens of American dollars.

And now, back to our story.

I ran out to my truck and grabbed a copy and a Sharpie. I scribbled something profound on the inside cover like "Here's my book – read it" and ran back inside feeling pretty good about myself.

As I grabbed my chair, I noticed a set of hooves resting there. Attached to those hooves were legs and at the end of those legs was the screaming woman from the restroom sitting on a chair next to mine. She didn't look pleased. My beer was still there in front of the chair where her hideous hooves were resting. My friend was in deep conversation with Andrea while his girlfriend was listening. I reached over the woman's hooves to hand Terry the book. "Here you go, buddy!" I said a bit loudly, hoping that the angry woman would look up and realize her hooves were on my chair. She didn't look up.

"Hey thanks, Bro!" Terry exclaimed. "Man, I'm going to read this as soon as I get home! In fact, I'm going to read this every day for the rest of my life!" Well, he didn't quite put in those exact words, but he *was* pretty excited about it. As a matter of fact, he was so excited that he went back to talking with Andrea while I pondered the dangers of asking the mad woman to remove her hooves from my chair.

I looked at the woman. She was slender, blonde, and might have been pretty if not for the horrendous way her face was screwed up with an unknown and unspeakable rage. She was staring hard at her drink. I mean, real hard as if she was projecting her thoughts at it and those thoughts were, "I'm going to cut the throat of the first moron to bother me!"

Sadly, I was that moron.

I slowly leaned over and gently, oh so gently touched her on the shoulder. Her head whipped around and her evil, burning eyes glared at me with loathing, hatred, and maybe a wee bit of attraction. I say "attraction" because there was a gleam in her eyes but now I know that lustful gleams and murderous gleams look pretty much alike. With my kindest, most humble and quivering voice, I said, "Uh, Miss… could I have my chair back? I… I was sitting here."

The look of hatred she shot at me made me want to cower in a corner mewling for my mother, but my beer was still on the table and I like beer so I stood my ground. I had a surreal feeling that the entire bar was oblivious to my plight. All eyes were on Eric as he sang "Maybe The Devil" which was an appropriate song for the creature that was before me. I was facing an unspeakable terror alone in a sea of happy people.

"Fine!" she screamed as she flung her hooves from my chair. "Sit there, you sploinking quack-mole! Just sit there, you lousy flud!"

I grabbed my beer and decided that it was the better part of valor not to sit there. I looked around and noticed an empty chair next to Terry's girlfriend. Unfortunately, it was also directly across the table from the crazed creature from hell but there was nowhere else to sit, so I sat. "Look, I'm sorry," I said, "but, I…" Snapping her head at me with such force that the spittle from her foaming mouth flew in every direction, she snarled, "No! It's o-fludding-kay! Sit wherever the flud you sploinking please, you sploinking flack-squash!"

All eyes were on Eric and his guitar while it seemed as if I were completely alone without defense against this demon from the netherworld. It turned out that Terry's girlfriend was the only person in the bar to witness my plight. She came to my defense, saying in a soft, sweet voice, "I'm sorry, but he really was sitting there…"

The demon woman snapped her head and flashed a withering look at the innocent young lady. She then turned back to me and snarled, "I'm sick and tired of you people always coming to *my* side of town and taking over everything!"

YOU PEOPLE? YOU PEOPLE? What the heck did she mean by that? Drummers? Cigar smokers? Drivers of F150s? Ex-sailors? It took a few seconds for her statement to sink in. Then I realized that there might be a bit of a racial aspect to her behavior. I was shocked. Terry's girlfriend was shocked. I'm sure that if anyone had been paying attention to my plight instead of enjoying Eric Hisaw's performance would have been shocked as well.

I looked at the slobbering creature before me and thought *can such a person like this still exist?* A split second after that thought, I realized that I was actually more shocked that I would be shocked that someone would say such a thing. The fact that I was shocked caused me to realize that things have really changed around here. You see, I grew up in a time when such a statement would not be shocking. I grew up when being treated differently was simply a fact of life.

I remember a time when everybody knew their place. Us Brown folk wouldn't think of going to the North Side unless we were mowing lawns or washing dishes. Even rich Chicanos tended to stay put or move to Floresville. The wrong color on the wrong side of town usually meant that something bad was going to happen and no one had any sympathy for an idiot who thought he could go anywhere he pleased just because he lived in America. I'm not just talking about Mexicans getting beat up by kickers. Heck, there's many an Anglo who ventured into our side of town and left a few dollars and a few teeth lighter.

Now everybody didn't feel that way. It was sort of a collective thinking; "birds of a feather" or so to speak. It's a good thing that everyone didn't feel that way otherwise I'd be telling an entirely different story. Looking around at the crowd at Sam's, I saw a room that was filled with white and brown faces and I started to think how attitudes about all sorts of stuff have changed over the years.

My Dad saw a lot of changes in his day. When he first joined the Navy in World War II, people were often judged by their skin color and ethnicity. There was a distinct separation between blacks and whites back then regarding shipboard duties. Chicanos kind of moved between both worlds, tolerated but not fully accepted by either side. My Dad was on active duty during the Zoot Suit Riots when sailors and Chicanos took to beating each other up in Southern California. For his protection, he was restricted to the ship and was in the uncomfortable position of being both a sailor and a Chicano. What should he do? Beat the crap out of himself?

You'd think that with all of the racism in the service my Dad would never get anywhere in the Navy. Well he went on to become a diver, Damage Controlman, naval firefighting instructor, a chief petty officer, and winner of the Silver Star. He always said that two thirds of what he accomplished was through strength of will and hard work. The other third was through the support of officers and NCOs who looked at him not as a minority but as a sailor. Now that doesn't mean that everything was hunky-dory. Heck, a little bit before I joined the Navy, there were race riots aboard the USS FORRESTAL and the USS MIDWAY.

Admiral Elmo Zumwalt who was the Chief of Naval Operations in the 70's truly believed that all sailors bleed navy blue regardless of race and started a reeducation program which required us to go through cultural awareness workshops. He ordered that all mention of race or ethnicity be purged from all service records and selection for advancement be based solely on merit and exam scores. I got to see a lot of changes during my twenty years of active duty. What I saw I liked because, even though there were still a few knuckle draggers out there, I was judged on how well I performed my duties. I was sometimes judged on how I looked but that was only during personnel inspections.

The one thing about the service that tended to bring us all together was music. Beer also brought us together but that was probably because we were almost thrown in the brig after brawling with some Australian sailors in Western Samoa. Music just naturally makes you forget stuff because you're thinking of the song, the story it tells, and the lovely melodies of death metal or whatever it is that strikes your fancy. You don't care what the musician looks like as long as the music's good.

You know, musicians were segregated at one time but there were a few musicians that didn't care for all that nonsense. They wanted the best musicians in their bands regardless of color. Look up Eddie Condon, Benny Goodman, and Louis Armstrong. They were pioneers of desegregation. In fact, I strongly recommend picking the book, "Really The Blues" by Mezz Mezzrow a Jewish saxophonist in the 20's & 30's who once dated Al Capone's favorite hooker but stopped because he didn't want to hurt the feelings of such as nice, friendly guy. When he was sent to prison, he listed his race as "negro" so he could be in a good prison band. Nowadays it's nothing to see a mixed-race band. In fact, nobody even says "mixed race band" any more. A band is just a band and that's how it should be. It's the music that's important, not what the person looks like.

Yeah, I can kick back, close my eyes and listen to music for hours without a care in the world. I can hear a beautiful angel singing me a love song, making my lecherous heart all aflutter. The singer could have three eyes, two teeth, and a five o'clock shadow, but the only thing I see is an image of beauty cast by a song.

Speaking of good music and hideous women, my thoughts were snapped back to Sam's Burger Joint and the screaming banshee. "Sploinking, sploink!" she slobbered. Meanwhile, Eric Hisaw was crooning "…and tomorrow's a loooong way away." *You got that right, brother,* I thought to myself. I was miserable and then… I was scared.

Two hands, two large hands, two large manly hands placed themselves in a manly like fashion on the table between me and howling beast. "What seems to be the problem here?" asked the rumbling voice coming from somewhere above the scary hands. *Oh, Lord. I'm doomed. It's her boyfriend.*

Grendel's mother screamed, "This son of a biscuit-eater is a muddafludding flidsquish!"

Terry's girlfriend tried to save my skin and told him, "Sir, he was sitting there and she put her hooves on the chair when he went to get Terry a book and he came back and her hooves were there and he was nice to her but she told him that you people this and you people that and you people and you people and we're always coming to her side of town and she can't do anything on her side of town because we're on her side of town and please don't kill him, Sir!"

The large, manly hands slowly lifted off the table. *Mommy!* One of the large, manly hands placed itself on my left shoulder as I whimpered. "Oh, Dude," said the voice, "I'm so sorry man! She's not from around here. She's from Colorado."

"Huh?"

"Yeah, she does this all the time."

"Fine! Take his side!" screamed the harpy. "I'm out of here! I hate this place!" She stomped off, taking her venom outside, her hooves clicking down the street.

The kindly behemoth standing over me said, "Well, I better go before she starts eating kittens or something. I'm so sorry about all that."

"No problem."

The guy who didn't kill me left and I could only think how glad I was that things have changed so much nowadays. Everyone in the bar seemed happy. Eric Hisaw was singing, I had a cold beer in my hand, and all was right with the world.

7 TRUTH AND A FICTION

If you can't tell by now, my life's been full of interesting people, adventures, and unbelievable tales. The following stories cover all three. A Lucky Man is about being taught to appreciate the simple things in life. Where The Heck Is BETO is about an oasis on a tortuous road trip. El Pestoso is the true story of one of my descendants in another solar system who gets a lesson in explosive space food 800 years from now.

A LUCKY MAN

It's kind of hard to appreciate the small things in life when you're up to your neck in crap. I should know because in the summer of 2000 I was in the ninth year of in a twenty year stretch of bad luck. I was raising two boys and a girl on my own. My oldest son was going through his idiot phase where he hung out with other idiots which resulted in my picking him up at the juvenile detention center more times than I care to recall. My daughter was going through her "my world is Blackness and Pain" phase while simultaneously discovering boys. My youngest son was dealing with separation anxiety and anger issues which caused me no end of heartache. My neighborhood was filled with gang-bangers, wannabe gang-bangers, and unattended pit bulls roaming the street. I was cursed.

I got a house on the far west side of San Antonio close to three years before this story took place. I moved here when I retired from the Navy. I was alone with my three kids, broken hearted, and trying my best to build a new life for my family. I got a job working at Palo Alto College administering entrance exams to incoming students. It wasn't a bad job, but I had a lot of bills and struggled to make ends meet. Having to be both mother and father to three kids isn't easy. There are only so many ways you can make Dad-Burger Helper before it gets real old and you have a revolution on your hands.

My kids seemed to sense that I was having a hard time. One day they approached me and told me that I needed to get out and start playing my drums again. I took their advice and started playing with some bands. It felt good but juggling work, bands, and raising kids is pretty darned hard. A lot of people asked me how I did it. I really don't know. It was tough. For a musician, performing is a release from all the worries in the world. For me, however, my problems were always waiting for me when I got home, and I had to deal with them. Now mind you, kids are not problems. They are a gift and a responsibility. I had to figure out how to satisfy my needs and be a good father at the same time. Let me tell you, it ain't easy.

When you're in a situation like I was in, it helps to have a mother and brother to lend a hand. It also helps to have good neighbors. Jimmy Zuniga was a really good neighbor. He lived in the house to my right. He was a bus driver. He was pretty darned friendly and always was ready to hand me a beer when I needed it most. The thing was, we had different schedules and didn't get to see each other and hang out very often. He had a little dog named Bandit who once saved my daughter from being attacked by two pit bulls. He was torn up pretty bad but thankfully survived. He was one brave little dog.

The neighbor to my left was a guy named George. He was kind of a tall guy and thin. He wasn't skinny though because his thinness was offset by just a little tiny bit of a spare tire around the middle. He was a brown guy with long, straight black hair that had a few strands of grey mixed in. He looked about fifty years old, but he didn't have a fifty-year-old face. What gave away his age was the way he looked at you. There was kindness in that look. It was a look that said, "Hey, Brother, I know what you're going through. I've been there and done that. Don't worry, it'll get better." He always had a tired, but happy smile on his face like he had traveled a long, hard road and was just happy to be Home.

I don't think George worked. Every time I came home, I saw him sitting out front on a lawn chair drinking a Lone Star. He would always stand up, walk over to the fence and greet me with a hand shake and a smile. Every once in a while, when I wasn't gigging or doing Dad stuff, we would hang out by the fence and shoot the breeze. George was always asking me questions about how I was doing and the musicians I played with. I'm ashamed to admit this but I was preoccupied with my struggles at the time and never really bothered to learn much about him. George, on the other hand, wanted to know everything about me. Every time I got through talking with him, I felt like I had unburdened myself to a priest. I always felt good talking with him.

I lost count of all the times I stuffed my drums into my little Mazda Protégé for a gig with George watching me. "Gil," he would say, "you're a lucky man."

"What do you mean?" After all, my life seemed to be a constant struggle.

George would give me his knowing smile and tell me, "You have a good job, you get to play music with all sorts of bands, and you have three kids who love you." Now how was I to respond to something like that?

I remember '99 has being a pretty darned hot year. I also remember it as a pretty tough year for me filled with ups and downs. It was a real rollercoaster of a year. I was playing with a band called True Stories but outside of our gigs at Casbeers (at the time, it was one of SA's best music venues) we didn't make much money and money was in short supply.

One day, I got a call from the owners of Casbeers. I was told that Julianne Banks was booked to perform but her drummer wasn't available. They asked if I could fill in and they would provide me with a CD of her music. I never heard of her, but I needed the money since I was planning a trip to Minnesota, and so I said yes. I picked up the CD but it was one of her acoustic recordings with no drums, so I really had no idea of what to do.

As it turned out, the show went off without a hitch. I was paid a hundred bucks and Julianne asked me if I could drum for her anytime she was in town. I said, "Heck yeah!" and went to pack my drums back in my Mazda. As luck would have it, I noticed that both tires on the driver's side were slashed.

It wouldn't have been so bad if only one tire was slashed because I had a spare donut in the trunk. Sadly, I had two slashed tires and it was one in the morning. Lucky for me, one of the patrons lent me his donut that fit my car and I drove home with two donuts on the driver's side, the car leaning to the left at twenty-five miles an hour.

Steve and Barb (the owners of Casbeers) did the unheard-of thing of buying me two new tires the next day. I don't know of any bar owner who would do what they did for me. There's a special place in Rock-n-Roll Heaven reserved for Steve and Barb. I will always be grateful to them.

Naturally, I told George what had happened. I was ticked off about my tires getting slashed. George just smiled and said, "Gil, you're a lucky man. Someone lent you a donut and the bar owners bought you two new tires just in time for your trip to Minnesota." Damned if he wasn't right.

I drove up to Minneapolis prepared to jam with The Whitinos. Unfortunately, Brian the bass player was not available to jam so my best friend, Shawn, and I spent some time hitting the music scene. We saw some great bands like Doc's Mambo Combo featuring Michael Bland on drums. When we finally hooked up with Brian, we went to see Joe Juliano who really rocks.

Driving back from Minnesota, I noticed steam coming from my hood. I stopped somewhere in Oklahoma and noticed I had a leak in one of my hoses. I bought some duct tape and made my way back to San Antonio. By the time I got home, steam was coming out of all sorts of places.

Of course, upon arriving home, I told George about what happened, and he told me I was a lucky man. I got a great gig, had my tires slashed, been given new tires, didn't get to jam in Minnesota but got to see some great musicians, had my car almost blow up but made it safe and sound back home.

Even though I was a lucky man, I still needed to replace my radiator. Jimmy, my other neighbor, came over and said he'd help me. As is the story with any car problem, another neighbor came over to help. That guy was Danny who lived on the other side of Jimmy.

Danny knew everything about everything and said to me, "You don't need another radiator! The top is plastic. We can just seal it with liquid metal and it'll be as good as new." So, Danny pried off the top of the radiator, sanded down the inside of the top, slathered a bunch of liquid metal in the crack, let it dry, put the radiator back together, and everything was hunky-dory.

Naturally, George watched the proceedings and told me that I was a lucky man for having so many friends to help me out.

I soon got another call from Julianne who had a gig opening for Bob Schneider at The Lab. Bob was and is a great performer. We had a great show. We sat next to the stage while Bob was performing. We drank and talked and laughed a bunch. At one point, Julianne told me she wanted me to be her drummer. She asked me to move to Austin and would even cook for me. The bass player told me not to do it because her cooking sucked.

Well I started thinking that this was my big break. Julianne Banks was an up and coming musician who was making good money and I could have a real chance of playing full time while supporting my kids. I told her I'd think about it.

I told George all about it and he told me I was a lucky man.

One day, Julianne called me and asked if I could do a show in Austin for two hundred bucks. I naturally told her I would do it. Right when I hung up, my buddy Dave from True Stories called me and told me we had a gig that same day in Welfare, Texas for fifteen bucks. Welfare is almost the same distance from San Antonio as Austin. I was bummed. I needed the money, but True Stories was my band and I couldn't just split on them. I called Julianne and told her I had to cancel. I never played with her again.

As I headed to Welfare, I was thinking about the money I lost. I was heading up IH 10 and, right by Boerne, my check engine light came on, the temp gauge hit red and steam started coming from the hood of my car. I barely made it to the gas station on Ralph Fair Road when the car collapsed from heat exhaustion. I opened the hood and saw that Danny's infallible repair had sprung a few leaks.

I called Dave and told him I was stuck, and I wasn't even close to Welfare (welfare maybe, but not Welfare). John the bass player saved the day and picked me up. We loaded my drums in his van and we left my steaming car at the gas station. We headed out to Welfare. Dave told me that I was lucky I didn't do the show with Julianne in Austin because there's no telling where I would've broke down and I'd have had to cancel anyway.

Yep, I was darned lucky.

The dance hall in Welfare is really something. It's beautiful. The place is huge. It's all made of wood with a dance floor that can hold at least a couple of hundred couples. There's a second level with lots of seating that looks down on a stage that can easily hold a twenty-piece band. The bar is about a mile and a half from the stage, so you'd better get a few beers before you go on or you'll be worn out by the time you get your second beer. I don't know the capacity of that place, but I think it can hold several hundred people.

That night, we played in front of a massive crowd of about six people (not including the staff). They were spread out all over the place. The acoustics in the hall are fantastic. The band sounded huge. We rocked our asses off, earning every penny we got. It's really weird doing a great show and sounding like you're playing in Carnegie Hall and when you get done with a song you hear, "Clap. Clap. Clap. Clap. Clap. Clap." To be honest, that wasn't the worst crowd we ever had.

We used to do a regular gig at Red Hot and Blues in San Antonio. It used to be a great club. It was two clubs in one with a stage on the first floor for blues and a stage on the second floor for rock. It was taken over by some morons who got rid of the downstairs stage and tore up it's beautiful bar to make way for pool tables and video games. They charged cover only for people going upstairs to see the band.

Our gig was on Tuesday nights (the worst night on the planet to do a gig). I think our biggest crowd was three, including the bartender. Many times, we played for just the bartender. One night, even the bartender left the place. We kept playing anyway since we were getting twenty-five bucks apiece. After each song, we could hear a faraway voice scream out, "Yeah! You guys rock!" We didn't know where the voice came from since there was no one in the bar and the voice seemed to come from behind me.

It turned out that there were some big windows behind the stage that were kept open to let the smoke out. The voice was coming from the windows. After a while, we all went to the window and looked down. Down on the sidewalk was a wino in ragged clothes. He was looking up at us. He was smashed. He was waving and yelling, "You guys rock! You're the best band I ever heard!"

Dave yelled down at him, "Why don't you come on up?"

The bum yelled back, "They're charging cover! Why don't you tell them I'm with the band?"

John told him that we'd like to, but we couldn't do it. He replied, "You guys suck!" and walked off into the night.

So now you can see why the Welfare gig wasn't so bad. What was bad was after the gig. We had to pack my drums into John's already overloaded van and drive back to the gas station on Ralph Fair. By some miracle, my car started, and we loaded the drums in my pathetic vehicle. Since the night was cool, the car wasn't going to overheat as long as I drove real slow. I limped along at 35 miles per hour with the guys following me all the way to Loop 410. I finally made it home about 4:00 a.m. cursing my luck and Danny's handy work.

The next day I bought a radiator and put it in myself.

As I was working on the car, George came outside with two beers; one for him and one for me. He asked what happened and I told him the sad story. "You're a lucky man," he said, "You could've been stuck on the road to Austin with no one to help you."

Yeah, Dave and John told me the same thing. Lucky me.

About a week later, I was driving home after a particularly horrible day at work. Like I mentioned earlier, it was a hot summer. It was like a zillion degrees in the shade. The heat was just oppressive. Just stepping outside made my lungs seize it was so hot. I was miserable and depressed. I was broke, tired, and angry. I hated the world and my life. I turned up the AC all the way with the vents turned to my face to cool me off.

As I pulled up to the house, I wondered what new disaster was awaiting me. I saw George sitting out in the sun, sweating like a dog. As usual, he had a beer in his hand. He reached into his cooler to get me a beer. I didn't feel like talking to him. I was tired, hot, and pissed off.

He came up to the fence to hand me the beer. I was about to tell him that I was in no mood to talk. He smiled at me. His entire body was drenched with sweat. As he extended the beer to me he said, "Gil, you're a lucky man."

"What?"

He just smiled the same knowing smile he always had on his face and simply said, "You got air conditioning."

I stopped in my tracks. Those four words brought me to reality. Here was a guy who didn't have a lot. I had no idea what kind of life he led. He didn't have much, but he appreciated everything he had. He didn't have money, but he was always willing to offer me his last beer.

I realized right then that despite all my trials and tribulations, I had things that some people don't have. I had experiences that some people can only dream about. I have friends who care about me. I have a family that loves me. I have a talent that allows me to do the things that I love. I have air conditioning.

I am a lucky man.

WHERE THE HECK IS BETO?

Most everyone who knows me knows that I go up to Minnesota quite a bit. The trip is very therapeutic for me. I visit two of my best friends Shawn and Brian. We have a band called The Whitinos and we hang out in the basement writing songs, jamming like crazy, and angering the neighbors. I've driven up there around eight times since '98. The drive to Minneapolis from San Antonio is pleasant. There's absolutely no scenery, no mountains, and no excitement to be had on that drive. That's the way I like it.

My Minneapolis trips are supposed to be relaxing and filled with music. The drive both ways is usually very relaxing. It's an easy trip because IH 35 runs from SA straight to my destination. I like to leave San Antonio about 4:00 a.m., take my time, stopping frequently at rest stops or restaurants I haven't eaten at before, and arrive in Emporia Kansas in the early afternoon. I hit the sack about 7:00, wake up at 4:00, have a good breakfast, take off about 5:00 and arrive in Minneapolis around ten hours later. I'm still fresh and ready to party with my friends.

There was one particular trip that didn't quite go as planned. My kids went by bus to visit their mom in San Diego a couple of days before I was to leave. There were delays and they wound up in the wrong place. Needless to say, I was getting pretty panicked and called every possible stop trying to find them. They finally arrived in San Diego about five hours before I was planning to leave for Minnesota. I was pretty worked up and couldn't sleep. I didn't take off until 7:00 a.m., which threw me totally off schedule.

The ten-hour drive to Emporia turned into twelve hours and was hell on wheels for me. What should have been a nice, relaxing drive turned into a journey of mind-numbing monotony. Miles and miles and miles and miles of endless flat grabbed my already exhausted brain and slowly squeezed it into a handful of mewling mush. I'm not kidding. Have you ever seen real flat? I mean, flat isn't so bad when you're driving down the road, listening to music, and at peace with the world. But when you're dead tired and have countless miles to get to your destination… well then flat's just plain torture.

My '94 Mazda Protégé was a zippy little car. Her red paint was faded and chipped in spots but she really handled the road well. I think the fact that she had a 5-speed manual transmission kept my mind somewhat alert and prevented me from nodding off. It was with great relief that I arrived in Emporia.

I like staying in Emporia because they have a ton of motels and just as many places to eat. It's a real clean town. There's something about it that feels safe. I only stop to spend a night and move on but it's one of those places where I just know nothing bad is going to happen. So, I was quite put off when I saw a "No Vacancy" sign at the first motel I came to.

As I continued down the main drag, I looked around and, as far as I could see, "No Vacancy" signs were blinking. I kept driving around and nowhere could I find a vacancy. Every cheap motel was booked. I was so tired I didn't care if I paid $100 for a room. I just wanted to sleep. Even the expensive places were booked. I finally asked someone why there were no vacancies anywhere and I was told that there was a big state softball tournament in town and there was no chance in hell that anyone could get a room in Emporia for the next couple of days.

I wanted to cry.

I had driven around for an hour looking for a room only to find disappointment at every stop. Finally, at 9:00 p.m., I got back on IH 35 praying to God that I'd find a place to stop. I knew that between Emporia and Kansas City (108 torturous miles away) lay a barren wasteland of Nothing. I steeled myself with three cups of coffee knowing that I'd probably not get in a bed until after midnight and I would more than likely fall asleep at the wheel and be killed in a violent explosion when the Mazda would slam into a gasoline truck, vaporizing me, my drums, and all identification so no one would know who to notify thereby leaving people to wonder if I had finally run off with Maria Conchita Alonzo or Daphne Zuniga.

Driving in Kansas at night while trying to stay awake can be really scary. It's like really, really dark out there. There's nothing to keep the mind distracted. There's only dark. There's only flat. That night there was only dark and flat illuminated by the Mazda's headlights. The only sound besides the breeze blowing through the car windows was that of the wailing and gnashing of my teeth. I must have prayed to over four hundred gods for a resting place until I realized that God may be just a wee bit perturbed with that kind of sacrilege so I returned to my wailing to the Holy Trinity and all of the saints and future saints.

I was only about twenty minutes out of Emporia when I realized there was no way I was going to make it to Kansas City. I started to look for a relatively safe spot on the side of the road to park and get murdered in my sleep. Then, for some reason, I started thinking about my Uncle Beto. His real name was Roberto but, in my neck of the woods, anyone named "Roberto" is always nicknamed "Beto." I couldn't get him off my mind and it bothered me. It was such a strange thing to be thinking about. I guess it made me a bit more alert.

BETO flashed in my mind.

BETO flashed again.

BETO. BETO. BETO. BETO. BETO. BETO flashed over and over again. I realized that, in my mind, BETO was flashing in blue neon. It was really strange that Beto's name should be flashing in blue neon. What was even stranger was the word "MOTEL" also flashed by his name. I started to slow down because I was fascinated by this hallucination. Here on a dark road in the middle of Kansas, in the dead of night, the words "BETO" and "MOTEL" were flashing in blue neon. Another word flashed below BETO and MOTEL. That word was: VACANY

I don't know when I snapped out of my stupor, but a voice in my head said, "Hey, pendejo! That's a stinking sign! That's a stinking motel! There's a stinking vacancy!" It only fleetingly crossed my mind to think that the middle of Kansas is a strange place for a Mexican named Beto to have a motel. I didn't care though. All I knew was that God wasn't very busy at the moment and thought maybe He'd give this poor slob a break. I slammed on the brakes and made a hard-right turn toward the sign. As I made the turn, I noticed a sign that said, "BETO JUNCTION" which I found passing strange.

The nice lady at the counter was probably a bit shocked to see a wild haired, crazed Brown guy with dark circles around bloodshot eyes, wearing torn jeans and a coffee stained sleeveless t-shirt rush up to her waiving a fistful of dollars and gasping, "I need a room. I don't care where. Smoking or non-smoking is fine." I'm probably lucky she didn't call the cops. Then again, maybe she was used to seeing crazed, wild eyed travelers begging for rest.

When I saw my room, I thought I was in Heaven. There… right there against the wall was the most beautiful thing I had ever seen in my life. It was a bed, a *real* bed, not some hallucination. I dropped my bag by the door. I just had enough strength to wash my face and brush my teeth before hitting the sack. As I stripped to my skivvies, I noticed there was a shiny new penny in the middle of the bed. It had to be a lucky penny. I picked it up and placed it on the night stand. I crawled into bed, turned off the light, and just as I was nodding off I whispered, "Thanks, God."

I woke up at 5:00 a.m. after seven of the most restful hours of sleep in my hazy memory. I jumped in the shower, figuring I'd better hurry so I could find a place to eat. I started wondering just who was this Beto guy, why did he build this motel, and how did the junction come to be named after him. I figured maybe he was a vaquero from the 1800's who wound up in Kansas and settled there. His descendants were probably still running the motel and I definitely wanted to thank them for giving a weary traveler a place to rest.

The motel office was closed when I left so I placed the key in the slot provided for early check-outs. I walked to the car prepared to drive an hour or so before I could eat when I realized there was a gas station just yards away. Then I noticed there was a trucker chapel right by the gas pumps. I kid you not. And then I saw the BETO JUNCTION RESTAURANT. Holy moley! Beto obviously built himself a nice little oasis. His descendants were probably making a killing from the looks of all the cars and big rigs that were parked all over the place. I guess I was too tired to notice this stuff when I parked at the motel.

I filled up my car at the pump, parked, and walked into the restaurant. As I sat down, I noticed a small BETO JUNCTION newspaper lying next to the salt and pepper shakers. I asked the pretty waitress for a menu and she told me the newspaper *was* the menu. Sure enough, I opened the newspaper and there was the darned menu. Everything sounded good to me but, since I was hitting the road, I ordered a coffee, small orange juice, two eggs over easy, hash browns, and toast.

As I sat eating what was a perfect breakfast, I noticed something funny. For a place where everything was named after a guy named Beto, there sure weren't many brown faces around. In fact, I was the only brown guy in all of Beto Junction. I called one of the waitresses, who was wearing a WHERE THE HECK IS BETO JUNCTION t-shirt over and asked her, "So who's this Beto guy this place is named after?"

She looked at me with beautifully confused blue eyes and replied, "Who?"

"You know. Beto. The guy this place is named after."

"Beh…," she began and then I could almost see a light bulb go off in her pretty little head. "Oh! You mean BETO!"

"Yeah, that's what I said."

She shook her head and said, "No, you're pronouncing it wrong. It's pronounced 'BEE-TOE' BEE-EE-TEE-OH, BEE TOE!"

"Huh?"

She pointed to the top of the newspaper menu and showed me that BETO Junction was actually B.E.T.O. Junction where the highways from Burlington, Emporia, Topeka, and Ottawa intersect. She smiled and walked back to the kitchen to tell everyone about the moron sitting at the counter.

I guess it's safe to say I was a bit disappointed to find that the place wasn't named after a guy named Beto. It didn't bother me too much though because I was rejuvenated and ready to hit the road again. My next stop would be Mason City, Iowa which happened to be the home of my favorite toilet with the automatic shredding seat cover.

BETO Junction was miles behind me when the sun started to rise. I was wide awake and refreshed. I thought it'd be nice if there really was a vaquero named Beto who settled there. It would've made a neat story. Then again, it's still pretty neat that God placed BETO Junction right where I needed it to be.

EL PESTOSO - A tale of futuristic terror and human triumph or something

2850 A.D.

There are times when one is forced to believe in Fate. We want to believe we're the masters of our destinies. We choose to be happy rather than wallow in pain and sorrow and yet we often have red hot pokers crammed up our collective grasses more times than we care to remember. My good friend, Fredo, didn't believe in Fate. I tried to warn him, but The Great Poker of the Universe was heading for him at warp speed.

Fredo "El Pestoso" Sanchez and I come from Nemroy, the twelfth planet of the Garlef System. The native Garlefians still consider humans as outsiders even though we've been there for a hundred years. They call us Pash Nefoont which, according to my parents, means "Star Masters." But my Garlefian classmates told me it really means "Dick Heads."

I first met Fredo when he moved in with his aunt Socorro after his parents were killed. Everyone said they died in a particularly hideous manner. What was worse, Fredo was there when it happened and he was strangely affected by the incident. How he was affected, no one knew for sure, but it had to be something awful. Adults refused to tell us kids what happened so rumors spread about the drooling, cross-dressing, masochistic twelve-year-old that was moving into the neighborhood.

Fredo's flight arrived at Slackjaw Spaceport and I was there to meet him because my Dad was a family friend. I, for one, was nervous about meeting with the Unknown. As it turned out, my fears were unfounded. Fredo looked pretty normal to me. As we went to greet him, everyone seemed to suddenly look ill. They were all coughing and gagging. Except me.

"Hijo! Que peste!" exclaimed my Dad. "Quien tiro el pedo?"

Well I knew that I wasn't the one who threw the fart. It was probably Uncle Beto. He was always farting. It didn't bother me since I had a cold and couldn't smell anything any way. But the coughing and gagging got worse as Fredo drew near and, from the redness of his face, I suspected it was he who had farted.

It turned out that Fredo didn't fart at all. He just plain smelled like a cabbage that had been fermenting in someone's grass for a month. I was the only one who could be near him that first week, so we quickly became friends. And then I got over the cold.

As my sense of smell returned, I understood why everyone gagged when Fredo came near. Soon, everyone in the barrio started calling him "El Pestoso" (The Stinky One), including his Aunt Socorro. Poor Fredo was obviously hurt by the name-calling and the fact that no amount of bathing could lessen the smell. It took almost two years for the stench to fade. He was my friend though and I stood by him. I guess that's why he told me how his parents died.

It turned out that they were killed while working the Front at the beginning of the Teronic War. Many people believe the Terons killed Fredo's parents and that's why he joined the United Planetary Uniformed Response Service. It's true that they were killed, but Terons didn't kill them. Revenge was not the primary motivation in his joining the service. I think Stupidity caused him to take the oath of enlistment.

Weeks after the war started, Fredo's parents, Bernie and Josefina Sanchez, decided it was their patriotic duty to provide for the fast food needs of our troops. The fact that they would make a killing selling overpriced crap to fellow patriots only fleetingly crossed their minds. They converted Bernie's old Cholo '35 Star-Bus into a mobile canteen, stocked it with snacks from a dozen systems, packed up their young son, and headed to the Front.

B & J's Mobile Canteen was popular throughout the Hoek Quadrant. Affectionately known as "The Roach Coach" by our troops, it catered to the fast food needs of many species. This can be quite dangerous if one samples the wrong interplanetary fare.

The BJ Burger, named after Bernie and Josefina, was a favorite of every being. The troops just called it the BJ, which Bernie didn't appreciate. I suppose having one's wife take an order of a "BJ to go" from every male in the quadrant would eventually get on one's nerves.

On the day of his parents' demise, Fredo had to go to the bathroom. The Roach Coach's waste tank was full, so he used the Port-A-Crapper LS which was behind the canteen. That his life was spared because he had to use a different toilet had to be due to the Hand of Fate. If not for the Port-A-Crapper LS there would be no story for me to tell.

While Fredo was taking a crap, a Lageshian Intestoid Being

approached The Roach Coach. It had just received news that its spouse had slithered off with a proctologist and now it wanted to commit suicide. It solemnly ordered a Super Double Bean & Cheese Burrito and a Dr. Pepper.

Bernie, being unaware of the danger in serving potentially explosive foods to a Lageshian Intestoid Being, took the money and shoved the burrito and Dr. Pepper down its pulsating food opening. The resulting explosion doomed not only the Intestoid, but the occupants of The Roach Coach as well. The screams were incredible. The screams are always incredible when one is downwind of the now famous Stinking Pit of Hoek.

The Port-A-Crapper was thrown fifty yards from ground zero and was buried under a pile of unspeakable ooze. Fredo's screams could barely be heard over the horrific fits of gagging from the onlookers. It wasn't until a biohazard cleanup team arrived that he was pulled from the insidious remnants of the explosion.

It's hard to imagine that anyone could survive such trauma but, if Fredo could live with it I certainly could live with being his friend. Even after his stench faded and people started hanging with him we remained best buddies.

People still called him "El Pestoso" but didn't remember how he came by that name. One thing for sure, his farts were famous not only in our barrio but in all of Nemroy. Socorro would often say, "Mijo, I don't think anyone has farted like that since the First Migration!"

My grandfather told me horrendous stories of the First Migration and the settlement years that were passed down to him by his great grandfather. I don't know how my ancestors survived the five-year transit to Aztlan (which is the capitol of The League of United Latino Planets) in deep space with nothing to eat but beans and tortillas. The stench in the ships must have been overpowering. It is a historical fact that beans were outlawed on Aztlan for fifty years after the colonists arrived.

The Second Teronic War started soon after Fredo and I turned eighteen. He immediately suggested that we join UPURS Space Navy and go kill a few of those purple, giggling dinosaurs. "No way," I told him. "Heck, I hate those pinche lizards too, but UPURS is already muy chingon as it is and two more Chicanos in uniform ain't going to help them anyway."

"Chingado," Fredo responded. "Do you think I hate Terons? Shoit no! I just want to get away from here!"

Well, I was still Fredo's friend and I wasn't about to desert him so I enlisted too. Except for boot camp, it wasn't too bad at all. We had nice uniforms, the pay was good, and we partied like idiots.

We got our orders to the space frigate UPSS MARVIN SHIELDS (SF-1066), which was in the Spanky Quadrant. Our homeport was on the planet Squeed in the port of Roseanne. The ship was in dry-dock when we reported. When Fredo saw who our shipmates were, he got the biggest shoit-eating grin on his face that I ever saw.

"Holy shoit, man!" Fredo exclaimed. "It looks like we're the only humans onboard!"

He was right. There were Moldarian Spittlemen, Safronite Crabbies, Antarian Rantry-Squeezers, and even Vegan Intelli-Nads. As we looked around the ship, we saw beings from almost every intelligent race in the free system. This was a dream come true for Fredo.

"Finally. Finally, I'm not the only weirdo. Damn, Bro! Isn't this great?"

Yeah, great. A great big pain in the grass, I thought. Now I don't think anyone could call me bigoted by any stretch of the imagination, but there's just so much weirdness a guy can take. Only a person who's served in the UPURS can possibly understand what it's like living day in and day out with a whole pile of alien species. I mean you can get used to almost anything if you're around it long enough, but some things you never get used to.

You see, the Rantry-Squeezers aren't so bad once you get used to the screams of the rantries. Crabbies pretty much stick to themselves and don't bother anyone except for the occasional curse. The Intelli-Nads can get a little creepy since they communicate by touch. It's the Spittle-Men that really bug me because I can't talk with one without wearing a raincoat and goggles.

None of the aforementioned beings were even remotely as repugnant as the slithering thing that reported for duty last year. I remember walking topside with Fredo and being hit by a horrendous stench. I hadn't smelled anything like that since the day I got over my cold when Fredo became my friend.

"I smell something familiar," Fredo said.

"Me too and I don't want to know what it is."

Standing or laying or something or the other by the Officer of the Deck was what could only be described as a poop-sleeve with arms. It looked something like a large, pulsating, pinkish meat tube. At the top of the tube was a gaping hole, which I assumed was its mouth. Below the mouth were fifteen eyes set around the tube like a nightmarish necklace.

It had four arms which were somewhat like those of a salamander but long enough to reach both ends of its quivering body. Those arms seemed to be in constant motion, rubbing the length of its body with a disgusting, gelatinous substance that continually oozed from its insidious, gaping maw. To my horror, the OOD was calling me to the Quarterdeck.

"Hey, Polanco! Get yer stinkin' human azzomocule over here before I rip yer head off and shoit down the hole!"

I double-timed it to the Quarterdeck and stood at attention, scared shoitless. The OOD was a seven hundred-pound Betan Beastman and I have seen him rip heads off and shoit down the holes several times. Let me tell you, there was no way I was going to cheese him off.

The OOD pointed at the being. "You know what this is?"

"No sir!" I responded as quickly as I could.

"This, you lousy wog, is a Lageshian Intestoid Being. It has volunteered for service in the greatest fludding space navy in the universe and you are going to get it a rack and show it around the ship."

Just fludding great. I was stuck babysitting a giant, fludding intestine. Things couldn't possibly get any worse.

Fredo was laughing. "Isn't this fludding great? I always wanted to meet an Intestoid. Shoit, we can put it in the top rack over you. Come on, man! It's almost liberty call. Let's get in our civvies and show it around town!"

I whispered to my friend, "Hey, man. What the flud are you talking about? That's an Intestoid! Have you forgotten that your parents were

135

killed by one?"

"Yeah, but this Intestoid didn't do it. Besides, its odors bring back memories."

Well Fredo was my friend and I guess it couldn't hurt to be nice to the stinking thing. After a while the three of us became quite close.

Now FfFttT, as it was called, wasn't a bad Intestoid as Intestoids go. Once you get past the smell, it was a darned pleasant being to hang with. The conversations were kind of strange though since the language of Lageshian Intestoid Beings consists of rumblings, gurglings, and mild gaseous eruptions not unlike human flatulence. After a while you can actually keep yourself from gagging. You don't even want to throw up, because Intestoids think it's a compliment and will excrete what can only be described as Cocoa Puffs and Almond Joys swimming in brown gravy.

The thing that bugged me the most was that Fredo had taken a real shine to FfFttT. He seemed almost obsessed with learning everything about it. He found out that its father was assassinated in the Hoek Quadrant by a Mexican terrorist running a mobile canteen.

This was bad. I tried to convince Fredo that maybe we shouldn't get so chummy with FfFttT, seeing that it was the spawn of the Intestoid that killed his parents. Fredo wouldn't listen and insisted that we let bygones be bygones. I just knew something bad was going to happen.

One morning at muster, Chief Strain informed us that we would be getting underway the next day to engage the Terons. Poor FfFttT was scared. A scared Intestoid is not a pretty thing to behold. In fact, it's pretty darned sickening. Only the strongest stomachs can encounter a scared Intestoid and live to tell the tale. Fredo said he would take it below and calm it down.

I had the first watch so I couldn't follow them. When I was finally relieved, I went down to the berthing compartment. When I got to my rack, Fredo and FfFttT were nowhere to be found. Fredo left a note on my locker. I felt a chill.

Gil,

FtFttT is really nervous so I'm taking it for a walk.
Chief says there's a roach coach on the beach. We're going

to get some chilidogs and a few Cokes. We'll bring some
back for you.

Fredo

I ran to the Quarterdeck as fast as I could. I had to get off the ship
and stop them. I didn't give a shoit if I got busted for jumping ship. My
friend's life was at stake.

Chief Strain was on the Quarterdeck. Just as I reached the brow, he
yelled, "Hey! Where in the flud do you think you're...?!!!"

The sheer force of the explosion was mind-boggling. We were
knocked off our feet. A split second later, we were covered by a thin layer
of unspeakable ooze that smelled like a cabbage that had been fermenting
in someone's grass for a month.

I looked up and could see the greenish mushroom cloud a quarter-mile
away. It was beginning to dissipate. The screams were incredible. The
screams are always incredible when one is downwind of the now famous
Stinking Pit of Roseanne.

8 SERIOUS CUSSING

This is the section that parents shouldn't let little kids read if they don't want them to learn bad words. I generally try not to cuss because my parents didn't like it at all. My Dad was a retired Navy chief petty officer and I can honestly say that I've heard him say bad words maybe a handful of times and that was only after I learned to cuss from my friends. I don't cuss in mixed company (for you young folks, that's whenever women or children are present) and I don't cuss in most of my stories out of respect for my parents and my handful of readers. But cussing is a part of life and sometimes can't be helped. Sometimes it's necessary to properly convey an emotional tale.

Peanut Butter and Jelly is about an incident in Minnesota where I was investigated for child neglect by a government agency run amuck. I'm the type of parent that tries to teach his kids right from wrong, provide for them what I can, and give them all the love in my heart. When I make a mistake, I try to fix it and learn from it because I know that I don't know everything, but the sheer stupidity and ignorance of the investigation completely destroyed my self-restraint. I cussed like a maniac. It definitely had a lasting effect on my opinion of government agencies.

The Stupid Racists is about my encounter with some stupid racists in Seattle. Yes, they were White guys but, as you have probably surmised, I don't generally think of White guys as racists since most Whites don't behave in a racist manner toward me at all. Heck, I've met racists of all colors, even Brown. I don't equate racism with a color. Rather, I equate racism with the ignorance and stupidity of individuals. The event I describe is about four ignorant and stupid guys wanting to beat me up because I'm Brown. It's one of the few times I've ever felt real fear because of my ethnicity. Each moment is forever etched in my mind and, as I wrote the story, every word and emotion came rushing back. Fear, survival, anger, and hatred filled every fiber of my being. The cussing just came out naturally and I find it necessary for this story.

PEANUT BUTTER AND JELLY

I'm a dad. I'm a grandpa. I have three kids and seven grandkids. I love them dearly. Like most parents, I want what's best for my kids. What I think is best for my kids doesn't always have to do with the best clothes, toys, or food. What's best for my kids is teaching them right from wrong, respecting people, religion, doing the right thing, discipline, new things, being a good person, and most of all, learning to love. Not every parent feels the way I do, and I respect that.

I know that some parents believe in giving their kids everything. They make sure their kids never want for anything. They praise everything they do. The parents are the children's servants. When they do wrong, they are told, "Please don't do that" or "let's talk about this." When the kids keep acting up, they're given a "time out." When their behavior gets worse, they're given the treatment known as "rewarding good behavior." When their behavior gets out of control an "intervention" takes place with the parents and a child psychologist who tells them what they're doing wrong. I've been told that this is the nurturing parenting method. Many kids brought up this way turn out to be assholes.

There are others who believe in strict discipline over nurturing. They give the child the bare minimum for survival. They're chewed out for the slightest thing. When they succeed at anything they're told, "Well it's about time!" They're taught to serve the parents. When they do wrong, they're locked in a closet, whipped with a belt, slapped, beaten, or worse. This is abusive parenting. Many kids brought up this way have problems adjusting in society. Unless they're taken out of that environment, they stand a good chance of becoming assholes like their parents.

I would venture to think that there are many kinds of parents in between the two extremes. Most are almost dead center, adjusting their methods according to their children's needs and behavior. Sometimes they're rewarded. Sometimes they're lectured. Sometimes they're praised. Sometimes they're punished (yes, I said "punished" which is different from "abused"). Sometimes they're smothered in kisses. Sometimes they're spanked (yes, I said "spanked" which is different from "beaten"). Some of these parents are good, some are bad, and some are just so-so.

Most parents do a decent job of raising their kids. The few that don't raise their kids properly either need a little help or need some jail time. Child protection agencies were created to help or protect kids being raised in a bad environment. Just like parents, some agencies do a good job, and some go overboard. In 1992, I had an unfortunate run in with a child protection agency run amok.

I was stationed in Minneapolis on shore duty and after staying in Richfield for a while, I moved the family to Bloomington. I really liked the area because it was clean, and everyone was very nice. The elementary school was close by. The kids really liked the place. I didn't think anything was strange until we made a new acquaintance.

This new acquaintance was a single mom with two daughters. The teenaged daughter was pretty and definitely had a bad reputation. There were constant parties at the place with lots of sex going on. The eight-year-old had a potty mouth and constantly cursed her mom. I remember the mom telling me that parents in Minnesota are scared of their kids because the Child Protection Agency will be on their case for the slightest thing. I found that hard to believe. I told her that the Child Protection Agency is there to prevent abuse and disciplining a kid isn't abuse.

"Gil," she said, "you'd be surprised how they define abuse." She told me how spanking was illegal, and parents weren't even allowed to raise their voices to their kids because it was damaging to their "self-esteem" and anything that damaged self-esteem was abuse. The sad thing was, all kids knew this and quite a few brats took advantage of that knowledge. I felt sorry for her, but I couldn't believe that the government would create an agency that could hurt a parent's ability to raise a child properly.

I remember one Saturday being home alone with my youngest son, Eddie, who was just starting school. He was watching cartoons and I was sanding a table top in the basement. Little Ed came downstairs and asked if he could watch me work and I told him it was okay. After a while, he got a little hungry and bored and asked me if it was okay for him to make a peanut butter and jelly sandwich. I asked him if he needed help.

He ran upstairs and said, "I can do it, Dad!"

After a while, Little Ed came back downstairs with his sandwich and a cup of milk. He sat down on a bench and watched me work as he ate. I told him that the sandwich sure looked good and he replied, "I can make one for you too, Dad!" I said that it was okay, and I would have one later. After I finished what I was doing, I went upstairs and checked the kitchen for whatever disaster Little Ed left. To my surprise, the kitchen was clean, the peanut butter & jelly jars were put up, and the only dirty things in the kitchen were the butter knife, plate, and cup that Little Ed used. I rubbed his head, messing up his hair with one hand and told him he did a real good job. We sat and watched TV. It was a really good day.

About two weeks later, I received a phone call at the Reserve Center. It was the school nurse. She told me that Little Ed wasn't feeling well and needed to go home. I took off from work and picked him up in the nurse's office. The nurse was real nice lady. She told me what good boy I had, and I should be proud of him. I told her I was proud because he was a good kid. It turned out Little Ed had a cold and had to stay home for a couple of days. I think it was about three weeks after Little Ed got sick that I received another phone call.

"Is this Mr. Polanco?" asked a female voice.

"Yes, it is," I replied, "How can I help you?"

"I'm Ms. (blank) from Hennepin County Child Protective Services. I'm investigating a report of possible child neglect in your area and was wondering if I could ask you some questions."

I said, "I'm not sure how I can help you since I don't know of any kids being neglected in my neighborhood." I was thinking that the lady with the two daughters had been reported by the little brat. I wasn't going to say anything bad about her because I thought she was trying to do a good job.

"Mr. Polanco," continued Ms. (blank), "the possible neglect I'm investigating is in your own home."

"What?"

"Mr. Polanco, I'd like to stop by this evening to interview you and your wife if I may."

"Uh, sure," was the only thing I could say.

I was dumbfounded. I was in a state of shock. What in the HELL was this woman talking about? NEGLECT? Jackie and I took good care of our kids. We ate as a family together. We did things together. We went to church together. They never went hungry. I made them smiley face pancakes on Saturday mornings! I drove home and told Jackie what happened. She broke down crying. We sat and waited for the knock on the door.

When the knock came, I answered the door. Ms. (blank) was at the door and standing next to her was a police officer. What the hell is going on here?

"Hello, Mr. Polanco, I'm Ms. (blank) and this is Officer (blank). May we come in?"

I led them to the living room where Jackie and I sat on the sofa while Ms. (blank) sat in a chair across from us. Officer (blank) declined a seat and stood at parade rest next to the case worker. I was already pissed off that anyone would think that we neglected our kids but bringing a cop here pissed me off even more. What were the neighbors going to think?

Ms. (blank) opened a tablet and started firing off questions at us in a cold, clinical manner. She could've been a Gestapo hippy lady for all I knew. She asked our names, birthdates, hometowns, date of marriage, etc. Then she started asking personal questions. All during the questioning, I was wondering why in the hell were we being investigated for neglect and my patience had worn pretty thin.

"Ms. (blank), please stop right there," I said. "I want to know why we are being investigated for neglect."

"I can't give you that information, Sir."

"What do you mean that you can't give me the information?" I asked.

Ms. (blank) gave me a cold look and said, "Sir, you have to answer these questions. We will review the information you give us and then, when there is a hearing, you will be informed on the particulars of the investigation."

"Where did this complaint come from?"

"Mr. Polanco, I'm not allowed to give you that information."

I was getting really steamed by now. I looked at the officer and asked him, "Sir, am I under arrest?"

The cop said, "No, Sir. You're not under arrest. I'm just here to make sure that things don't get out of hand."

I looked back at Ms. (blank) and said, "If I'm not being placed under arrest, then I think that I should know what you're trying to accuse me of and how in the hell you got this complaint!"

"Sir, I can't tell you how…"

"You will tell me, Ms. (blank), or I will be going to your superiors!"

Ms. (blank) looked up at the officer for support. He just shrugged and said, "I think he's in his rights." At that she opened another folder, looked down at it and said, "The State of Minnesota mandates that any person responsible for the care and education of children immediately make a report if abuse or neglect is suspected.

"Every child who goes to the nurse for any reason must be interviewed by a qualified person to determine if any abuse or neglect is taking place in the home. Do you remember picking up Edward from the nurse's office?"

"Yes."

"Well before you picked him up, he was asked a series of questions and if any answer is 'yes' the child is asked to explain the answer. The child's explanation is discussed, and a determination is made whether to file a report. The interview with Edward showed him to be a pleasant and well-behaved child. I see that every question regarding physical or psychological abuse was answered with a no. All questions regarding neglect were answered with a no except one."

"And what question was that?" I asked.

She looked down at her folder and answered, "The question was 'Do you ever have to feed yourself?' To which he answered, 'yes' and when we asked for an explanation, he told us that he made a peanut butter and jelly sandwich."

"I remember that," I said. "That's the day I was working in the basement and he asked me if he could make a sandwich."

"That's right, Mr. Polanco. He related the entire story and he seemed really proud that he made his own sandwich."

I looked at her in disbelief. The officer looked at her in disbelief, placed one hand over his eyes and shook his head. I stood up, and said, "That's why you bring a cop to my house because my son made a fucking sandwich?"

"Sir, you don't have a right to talk to me like that."

"Ma'am, this is my home and I'll talk to you any way I fucking please! What kind of fucking morons are running your office? What kind of fucking place is this? You call my fucking work and tell my fucking officer in charge that I'm being investigated for possible child neglect because my son made a fucking sandwich?!!!"

"Mr. Polanco, I'm going to have to ask you…"

"No, Ms. (blank)! You're not asking me any more stupid, fucking questions! If you have any fucking legitimate reason for bothering my family, you'd better say it now and have this officer arrest me. If not, then I suggest you pack up your shit and get the fuck out of my house!"

The idiot case worker started to say something, but the officer placed his hand on her shoulder and said, "Ma'am, I really think we should go."

As Ms. (blank) headed out the door I told her, "You'd better fucking tear that report up and tell your superiors that they're a bunch of fucking idiots and they can shove that report up their collective asses for scaring me and my family and wasting my fucking taxes investigating why my son made himself a fucking peanut butter and jelly sandwich!"

The police officer, who stayed cool throughout the incident, shook my hand and said, "Sir, I'm really sorry for any trouble we've put you through.

I thanked the officer. He walked to his police car, turned around, and said, "A peanut butter and jelly sandwich." He shook his head and drove off.

I never heard from them again and I assume that my file was destroyed. I almost hope that it wasn't destroyed so people can look at my case and see that the zeal for child protection can sometimes be twisted and have a harmful effect on families especially when "abuse" and "neglect" are given all-encompassing definitions by idiot bureaucrats.

I'd like to note that the incident took place in the 1990's and things have changed a bit in Minnesota. I looked up some of the mandates that are currently in place in Hennepin County. The definitions of "abuse" and "neglect" are still a bit ambiguous but it seems like there are some checks and balances in place now to ensure that false or superfluous reports are not so easily made.

I wonder if Ms. (blank) still works in child protection. I wonder how she feels about peanut butter and jelly sandwiches nowadays.

THE STUPID RACISTS

In January of '79, I was on active duty and stationed aboard the USS MARVIN SHIELDS (FF-1066) which was going through an overhaul at Lockheed Shipyard in West Seattle. I had six months left on my tour and I was having a great time. I loved going to Seattle because it was (and is) a beautiful and fun city to visit. I hated staying in the temporary berthing where we lived while the ship was in dry dock so I was always out shooting pool West Seattle or bar hopping in downtown Seattle with friends. There were many times that I'd just go out alone and enjoy the city.

I liked to wake up early on Saturdays when I didn't have duty and go into town for breakfast at The Dog House. From there, depending on my mood, I'd just do a pile of things. I'd always take a coffee to-go and walk to the Seattle Center or to Pike Place Market or all the way down to the Elliot Bay Bookstore which is my favorite bookstore in the whole world. Now anyone who knows Seattle will tell you that my wandering about would take a lot of walking. I'd be out from morning until midnight. Since I didn't have a car at the time, I did much more walking than I do now. I was obviously in much better shape back then.

There were some mornings when I would get a cup of coffee, take the bus from the shipyard, get off on Alaskan Way and walk the three or four miles to The Dog House and really build up an appetite if it was a particularly beautiful day. The place I'd get off at was south of downtown Seattle in the industrial district. It's a great walk in the morning because nothing is going on. I always got a kick out of this one building that housed a paper company. On the side and near the top of the building was a painted sign that declared in big, bold letters: REAMS OF PLEASURE

Yeah, I know. I'm easily amused.

One Saturday morning, I headed out to Seattle. The day was clear day with a beautiful blue sky but it was pretty darned cold. My friend John had duty so I borrowed his leather biker jacket because it was warm and it looked cool. I had a pack of smokes and about twenty bucks to last me. After breakfast at The Dog House, I walked all over town looking at stuff and pretty much enjoyed the day.

I guess it was about 4:00 p.m. when I arrived at The Gibson House which was historically a kind of can-can place and famous for The Gibson Girls. It's no longer that kind of place but they had pretty bartenders and the piano guy knew a pile of great songs. I could sit for hours listening to that piano and drinking coffee or a more relaxing beverage. I did that day.

When I arrived at The Arirang Tavern, later at night, I had maybe about eight bucks left. That was okay, because both Hong and Peggy who worked the bar always liked to try out their Korean dishes on me so I knew I didn't have to buy any food.

I was pretty good at pool back then and would usually win regularly enough to keep me in beer all night long. I won a few beers and just had a blast listening to Mister Lee & His Magic Organ. Now Mister Lee was just Mister Lee on stage, but his Wurlitzer organ had a drum machine and when he played, he looked as though he was thinking, "Yes! I am Mister Lee! I am talent!" Some of the regulars started calling his act, "Mister Lee and His Magic Organ."

I don't know what time I left the tavern, but I know I was pretty darned drunk. I needed to get some fresh air and decided to walk to the water front. I was cold, drunk, and a little hungry. I made it to Ivar's Acres and Acres of Clams (mm… I love that place) by the ferry landing. I had just enough money for a cup of clam chowder. As I ate my clam chowder, I realized that I was dead broke and didn't have a way back to the shipyard. Ivar's closed. In fact, everything around me was closed. It was 2:00 a.m.

I started to walk.

I knew I was about three and a half miles from a warm bed. I didn't mind the walk because it helped me to sober up. I didn't worry about anything happening to me since the people in Seattle are pretty laid back in a college liberal sort of way. They always struck me as being French with American accents. They're quite peaceful as long as you don't get in the way of their coffee. Hmm, I'm actually like that myself, about the coffee that is.

Now a drunk sailor who is sobering up with clam chowder on a cold night wind is still a drunk sailor whose sense of fear and common sense are pretty much non-existent. I walked south on the deserted street. I could hear my footsteps echoing off the sides of the buildings and the squeaks of the leather jacket I was wearing. I forget what I was thinking about, but I know I was oblivious to the yellow sedan that slowly pulled up to my left with its lights off.

"Hey, you fucking spic!"

I tensed up and kept walking, keeping my eyes straight ahead. My peripheral vision told me there were four young white guys in the car. They were drunk and laughing. One of them yelled out, "You fucking Mexicans thinking you're so bad when you're in a gang! How does it feel when you're alone?" I didn't answer but I can honestly say that I didn't feel all that good at the moment. I was kind of peeved though since the closest thing to a gang that I belonged to was the U.S. Navy.

I kept walking, hoping they'd just leave. Their cursing got louder as the car kept pace with my quickening steps. I realized that they intended to hurt me. My mind raced. I had to find a way out of the mess I was in. I looked for some kind of escape route but there was none. I was in the middle of an extremely long block occupied by an extremely long building. There was no fence to climb and no window to jump through. I knew that running would signal my doom. I was stuck.

"Hey, you piece of shit! I'm talking to you!"

I'm not sure how to explain it, but time for me seemed to slow down even as the situation was spinning out of control. I was strangely calm as I thought to myself, *I'm gonna get the shit beat out of me no matter what I do so I might as well go down fighting. I'd better put down the clam chowder.*

"Let's kick his ass!"

I stopped and slowly bent down to place the chowder on the sidewalk. When I did that, I noticed that the motorcycle jacket was very constricting. *Damn! I can't fight in this! I can hardly move my arms! I'd better take it off.*

"We're gonna beat the shit out of you!"

I straightened up and faced the car.

All four car doors seemed to open as one.

I started to unzip the jacket. I was ready to meet my Fate. As I pulled the zipper down, one of the guys in the back seat screamed, "He's got a gun!" Suddenly all four doors slammed shut and, to my disbelieving eyes, the car peeled off, racing down the street. I stood there dumbfounded, holding the jacket as I watched the car speed away.

A sudden rage seized me. I dropped the jacket and ran after the car as fast as I could, all the while screaming, "Come back you fucking assholes!"

I ran almost two blocks after the fading lights of the car screaming, "You fucking assholes!" I picked up a rock or a brick or a bottle or something and threw it after the car. I was cussing in eight languages I was so pissed off.

A car came up and someone called to me, "Hey, buddy, are you all right?" I know I wasn't in my right mind because all I could do was look at the guy and scream out, "Yaaaaaaaaaa!" as I ran at his car. The poor guy freaked out and sped away leaving me behind. I guess the driver thought I was some kind of nut case and, at that moment, he was probably right. As he drove away, I threw him the finger.

I walked back to where I left the jacket. I picked it up but I didn't put it on. I left the chowder on the sidewalk because I was no longer cold or hungry. I had one cigarette left. I lit it, took a deep drag, held the smoke in my lungs and exhaled. I was no longer drunk.

Whenever I tell my friends about those morons, I always end the tale with me chasing after their car. Everyone laughs and someone will say, "Stupid assholes." What I've never told my friends is that there is more to the story. The reason I never tell the rest of the story is that people can get incredulous when they hear adventure after adventure from a guy they drink with. The rest of the story actually happened and it proved to me that Justice does exist and it sometimes has a sense of humor. Cross my heart.

I'm kind of a resilient guy and I soon put the incident out of my mind. About a month later, I was hanging out in Seattle without a care in the world. I stopped by the Gibson House for some piano music and beer. I was having a good time and didn't want to leave but I had planned to go to Pioneer Square and catch some live acts before going back to the ship.

I stopped by Nikko's Oriental Garden to watch the go-go dancers for a while. Leaving the place, I walked south on 4th smoking a cigarette. Turning west towards 1st Avenue, I was busy deciding where I was going to end the night. Suddenly, to my surprise, I heard some familiar voices.

"Hey, you fucking niggers!"

I froze in my tracks. I looked up and, close to 2nd Avenue, I saw a yellow sedan with four white guys inside stopped near two black guys who were backing away from the car. I thought to myself, what the fuck? Then time slowed down for what was probably the next forty seconds. I didn't have a stop watch and can't be absolutely precise on the timing but it went down like this:

00.00-White guy sticks head out of window and screams, "Fucking niggers!"

00.02-Four car doors open while the two black guys back up.

00.03-Four white guys step out of car cussing at the black guys

00.03-I'm frozen in my tracks and I think, "It's those same assholes!"

00.04-00.09-Lots of cussing is going back and forth

00.10-One white guy goes to open the trunk of the car

00.11-I think that maybe I'd better help even the odds and start moving toward the confrontation.

00.14-White guy pulls a crowbar from the trunk of the car and holds it up with his right hand.

00.15-I freeze. The black guys freeze.

00.16-The white guys laugh and slowly move toward the black guys.

00.17-One of the white guys yells, "We're gonna kill you niggers!"

00.18-I start to unfreeze and think, "I gotta help!" and start running toward the scene.

00.19-White guy starts swinging the crowbar. I slow down. Black guys back up.

00.20-Yee haw!!!!

00.21-Crowbar slips out of white guy's hand.

00.22-Crowbar hits the ground, slides, and stops at the feet of one of the black guys.

00.23-Everyone freezes. I freeze a half block away. Black guys look down.

00.24-Black guys look at each other. White guys look at each other. I look at everyone.

00.25-One black guy reaches down and picks up crowbar.

00.26-Black guy looks at crowbar and then looks at his friend.

00.27-Black guys smile and nod their heads up and down.

00.28-Black guys start to walk toward white guys. One of them says, "Yeah, mother fucker"

00.29-One of the white guys yells, "Shit!" and the white guys run to the car.

00.30-White guys reach car and start to take off.

00.31-Black guy with crowbar manages to break the passenger side tail light.

00.32-Car screeches to a stop when the light is broken.

00.33-Black guy with crowbar catches up to stopped car and starts bashing the trunk while his friend simultaneously reaches through the rear window to grab one of the white guys.

00.34-I hear what sounds like a little girl screaming, "Get away! Get away from me!" The screams are coming from the car which seems strange since I don't recall seeing any girls in the car.

00.36-Car peels out and doesn't stop because the black guys are in hot pursuit screaming, "Come back, mother fuckers!"

00.39-I stand on the corner watching the fading tail light and two shadows chasing the car. I laugh and think to myself, "What a bunch of stupid assholes."

00.40-I light another cigarette and walk to Pioneer Square for a night of good music. I'm smiling.

ABOUT THE AUTHOR

Gil Polanco lives in San Antonio, Texas with the mother of his children, a womanizing neutered cat, one farting dog, and a turtle of questionable upbringing. His bad reputation comes from his being a retired Navy man and an insufferable drummer. He dreams of saving the Universe by flying a Ford Escort 5000X Rocket Wagon armed with Soidflab E explosives straight into the Inexplicable Grey Hole while listening to "The Romantic Warrior" by Return to Forever. His literary influences include Homer, Hungry Coyote, Snorrie Sturulson, and Patrick McManus.